DOROTHY DAY

TERRENCE C. WRIGHT

Dorothy Day

An Introduction to Her Life and Thought

IGNATIUS PRESS   SAN FRANCISCO

Cover photograph:
Dorothy Day at Maryfarm, Easton, PA ca. 1938.
Courtesy of the Department of Special Collections and University Archives, Marquette University Libraries

Cover design by John Herreid

© 2018 by Ignatius Press, San Francisco
All rights reserved
ISBN 978-1-62164-157-5
Library of Congress Control Number 2017947370
Printed in the United States of America ∞

To my children,
Benedict Canty Wright
and
Rachel Day Wright

We cannot love God unless we love each other, and to love we must know each other. We know Him in the breaking of bread, and we know each other in the breaking of bread, and we are not alone any more. Heaven is a banquet and life is a banquet, too, even with a crust, where there is companionship.

We have all known the long loneliness and we have learned that the only solution is love and that love comes with community.

—Dorothy Day, *The Long Loneliness*

CONTENTS

ACKNOWLEDGMENTS

Many people have contributed to the completion of this project. I would like to thank the organization ENDOW (Education on the Nature and Dignity of Women) for its early support of this book. In particular I am grateful to Terry Polakovic and Madelyn Winstead for their support, criticism, and comments on an earlier version of the manuscript.

I also want to thank Saint John Vianney Theological Seminary for its support, particularly a sabbatical release, which allowed me to complete this project. More important, I want to thank my colleagues for their encouragement and the staff of the Cardinal Stafford Library for their assistance in my research. But most of all I want to acknowledge my seminary students, whose interest in Dorothy Day reinforced my commitment to writing an introductory book that would serve as a doorway to a deeper exploration of her life and work.

I am also grateful to Vivian Dudro at Ignatius Press, whose careful criticism and comments on the manuscript brought it to its completion.

Finally, I want to thank Susan C. Selner-Wright, who as a friend and colleague critiqued and proofed earlier drafts of the manuscript and supported me through the process. Even more important, as my wife, Susan continues to teach me every day about the importance of doing little things with great love.

PREFACE

If I have accomplished anything in my life, it is because I wasn't embarrassed to talk about God.

—Dorothy Day[1]

In a historic speech to the United States Congress on September 24, 2015, Pope Francis identified four Americans "who shaped fundamental values which will endure forever in the spirit of the American people". Two are well known: Abraham Lincoln and Martin Luther King Jr. The other two are not nearly so well known: Thomas Merton, a Cistercian monk, and Dorothy Day, a Catholic laywoman. Pope Francis described how Day's "social activism, her passion for justice and for the cause of the oppressed, were inspired by the Gospel, her faith, and the example of the saints" as he held her up as a model for the world to follow to give hope to the oppressed. For those unfamiliar with Dorothy Day, this book seeks to provide an introduction to the life and thought of the woman who many consider to be one of the most influential American Catholics of the twentieth century.

Dorothy Day (1897–1980), together with Peter Maurin (1877–1949), founded the Catholic Worker movement in 1933. Day was a writer, a public speaker, a convert, and

[1] Rosalie Riegle, *Dorothy Day: Portraits by Those Who Knew Her* (Maryknoll, N.Y.: Orbis Books, 2003), 77.

a mother. Her life and writings speak clearly to our contemporary experience. She has inspired countless numbers
of people to reflect on the Catholic Church and its role in
promoting a more just and peaceful society.

My own experience of Dorothy Day began when
I started reading the newspaper the *Catholic Worker* in
college. When I became a teacher I began using Day's
writings in my classes, and I still do. Part of my reason
for writing this introduction came from an experience I
had with two of my seminary students, who had studied Day with me. Both men had spent their summer
assignments at local parishes. One student told me that a
retired priest at his parish had told him how glad he was
to hear that they were studying a person who criticized
Church teachings, a "dissenting Catholic"—like Dorothy
Day—in the seminary. The other student commented that
he had had the opposite experience, that his pastor was
angry when he heard they had studied Day, a "dissenting
Catholic", at the seminary. My response was that I could
not imagine why either of them would have thought that
Dorothy Day dissented from the teachings of the Catholic
Church. Day never understood herself as a dissenter, and
in my reading of her I had always been inspired by her
fidelity to the Church. In this introduction I hope to show
this faithfulness and dispel the mistaken view that she was,
with one important exception, a dissenting Catholic. In
her pacifism, Day clearly dissented from the teaching on
what is known as just war theory, but she grounds this
dissent firmly in Scripture.

Many Catholics are selective in their embrace of the
teachings of the Church: some claim that the Church
is right about teachings regarding sexuality and abortion
but wrong or naive about privileging the poor or the
need for a just wage; others claim that the Church is right

about privileging the poor and the need for a just wage but wrong or out-of-date on sexuality and abortion. Dorothy Day, on the other hand, is a Catholic who thinks that the teachings of the Church are right about all of it. She supported the Catholic teaching on sexual morality as strongly as she supported the teaching on social justice, because she saw that all Catholic teachings arise from the loving message of Jesus Christ in the Gospel. She believed that the Church promoted and perpetuated this message through its teachings and the sacramental life. Day was not ignorant of or naive about the ways in which Catholics and the institutional Church can fall far short of these teachings, but for Day these failures did not diminish the truth of the message. Father Daniel Berrigan, S.J., wrote that Dorothy Day was an inspiration "by living as though the truth were true".[2] In an age when it is often easier, more convenient, or more popular to live as if the truth were *not* true, Dorothy Day continues to stand as a model and an inspiration.

In 1997 the late John Cardinal O'Connor of New York officially began the cause for Dorothy Day's canonization. In March 2000 her cause was officially accepted by the Vatican, and she was declared a "servant of God", the first stage in the lengthy process of canonization. In November 2013 Timothy Cardinal Dolan of New York, in fulfillment of the canonical requirement that a bishop promoting a cause for sainthood consult with local bishops, asked the U.S. Catholic bishops to endorse the cause for Day's sainthood. Many of the bishops used this as an opportunity to speak in favor of her cause, and the assembled bishops voted to endorse it.

[2] Daniel Berrigan, introduction to *The Long Loneliness*, by Dorothy Day (San Francisco: Harper and Row, 1981), xxiii.

Because of her life, her writings, and her political stands, Day remains a controversial figure, but she also serves as a challenge to Catholics and non-Catholics alike to reflect on Christ's call for us to serve the least of our brothers.

The aim of this work is to introduce readers to the life and teachings of Dorothy Day. The first two chapters present a brief introduction to her early life prior to the founding of the Catholic Worker movement. To appreciate fully the development of her social conscience and her conversion to Catholicism, this brief biography is necessary. The following chapters address her life as the eventual leader of the Catholic Worker movement and explore the rich social doctrine of the Church: a doctrine that shaped Day's thinking and that Day, in turn, helped to shape. This work hopes to encourage a deeper understanding of the Church's social teachings and to place Day's work within this context.

Day understood herself first and foremost as a writer, and this study will draw mainly from her own writings to present her ideas. These writings include her autobiographies (*The Long Loneliness, From Union Square to Rome, House of Hospitality, Loaves and Fishes,* and her autobiographical novel, *The Eleventh Virgin*); her articles from the movement's newspaper, the *Catholic Worker*; and reflections from her journals, diaries, and letters. Many of the books about Dorothy Day are written by those who knew her and worked with her. I write as one who never knew Day, and my knowledge of her comes mostly from her writings. In this work I allow, as far as possible, Day to speak for herself.

I also make use of several of the books and biographies written about Day and the Catholic Worker movement. In particular I am indebted to Mark and Louise Zwick's excellent work *The Catholic Worker Movement: Intellectual and Spiritual Origins*. For biographical information, I draw from William Miller's biography, *Dorothy Day: A Biography*, and Jim Forest's biographies, *Love Is the Measure* and *All Is Grace*. I also wish to acknowledge my debt to the work that Robert Ellsberg has done in publishing *The Duty of Delight: The Diaries of Dorothy Day* and *All the Way to Heaven: The Selected Letters of Dorothy Day*.

With regard to the social teachings of the Church, I will largely draw from the *Compendium of the Social Doctrine of the Church* prepared by the Pontifical Council for Justice and Peace at the request of Pope Saint John Paul II. This wonderful volume brings together in one place a complete summary and explanation of the Church's teaching on a wide variety of social issues. All readers interested in these issues will find the *Compendium* indispensable. This work also appeals to papal documents and publications of the United States Conference of Catholic Bishops to explain the Church's social teachings. Unless otherwise noted, all of the quotations from Church documents can be found on the Vatican website (www.vatican.va). All biblical quotations are from the Revised Standard Version, Second Catholic Edition.

Chapter One

THE EARLY LIFE OF
DOROTHY DAY

Childhood

Dorothy Day was born on November 8, 1897, in Brooklyn, New York. She was the middle of five children and had two older brothers, a younger sister, and a younger brother. Her father, John Day, was a journalist who worked mostly as a sports writer covering horse racing. He married Dorothy's mother, Grace, in 1894.

When Day was six years old, her family moved from Brooklyn to Oakland, California, where her father had taken a job. Three years later, on April 18, 1906, events provided Day her first experience of serving others when the city of San Francisco was devastated by an earthquake. The initial shock damaged the water system, and the fires that broke out could not be contained. After three days of trying to control the fires, officials had to resort to dynamiting entire city blocks to create a fire break. In those three days 700 people lost their lives and 250,000 people lost their homes and possessions. While Oakland also experienced the tremors, the destruction was not as bad, and many who had lost their homes in San Francisco sought refuge across the bay in Oakland.

While the eight-year-old Day was frightened by the destruction of the earthquake and fires, she also recalls feeling a certain joy in helping her mother aid the homeless refugees from San Francisco. This early experience helped to shape Day's later commitment to the poor and the dispossessed. The earthquake closed the newspaper that employed John Day, and he decided to move his family to Chicago to look for work.

Initially her father was unable to find a job, and Day had her first experience of poverty during this time. Her family lived in a tenement building in the city, and Day was so ashamed of her home that when she walked home with school friends, she would enter a nicer apartment building so her friends would think that she lived there. But it was in this situation that she was introduced to Catholicism through her friendship with her neighbors the Barretts. Kathryn Barrett was one of Day's playmates, and Day was very moved by Kathryn's mother's piety. She recalled:

> It was Mrs. Barrett who gave me my first impulse toward Catholicism. I went up to Kathryn's to call for her to come out and play.... In the front bedroom Mrs. Barrett was on her knees saying her prayers. She turned to tell me that Kathryn and the children had all gone to the store and went on with her praying. And I felt a warm burst of love toward Mrs. Barrett that I have never forgotten, a feeling of gratitude and happiness that still warms my heart when I remember her. She had God, and there was beauty and joy in her life.... Mrs. Barrett in her sordid little tenement flat finished her breakfast dishes at ten o'clock in the morning and got down on her knees and prayed to God.[1]

---

[1] Dorothy Day, *From Union Square to Rome* (Maryknoll, N.Y.: Orbis Books, 2006), 26.

Another friend, Mary Harrington, was the first to tell Day about the lives of the saints, and she loved these stories. Day was drawn to the spiritual truths that these lives expressed, and she tried to persuade her little sister that they should emulate the saints by being pious and sleeping on the floor. While these impulses may reflect a child's understanding of sainthood, Day maintains that "the thrill of joy that again and again stirred my heart when I came across spiritual truth and beauty never abated, never left me as I grew older."[2] Day was experiencing the beginning of her long search for God.

When her father finally found a good job, he was able to move his family to a nice house outside of the city. While committed to providing for his children, John Day spent little time with them. Despite this distance, her father did encourage his children in their education. He provided them with a library of classic literature, which his daughter loved and would read for the rest of her life. During these years Day joined a friend in attending an Episcopal church and began reading the Bible and, for the first time, *The Imitation of Christ* by Thomas à Kempis. After encouragement from the pastor, Day's parents permitted her to be baptized in the Episcopal church. But her religious life did not develop much beyond this point, and she turned her interests in a more worldly direction.

Around this same time Day's brother Donald began writing for a newspaper that focused on the plight of the working poor in Chicago. The more she learned about the history and the struggles of the workers' movement, the more she was drawn to it. Upton Sinclair's famous "muckraking" novel, *The Jungle*, about poverty, squalor, and inhuman working conditions in Chicago, further opened

[2] Ibid., 28.

her eyes to the plight of the poor. She also read Peter Kropotkin's accounts of poverty in Russia. Day recalled:

> Kropotkin especially brought to my mind the plight of
> the poor, of the workers, and though my only experience
> of the destitute was in books, the very fact that *The Jungle*
> was about Chicago where I lived, whose streets I walked,
> made me feel that from then on my life was to be linked
> to theirs, their interests were to be mine; I had received a
> call, a vocation, a direction to my life.[3]

Day was a good student, and when she graduated from
high school at the age of sixteen, she won a scholarship for
$300 to attend the University of Illinois at Urbana.

University Years

Dorothy Day entered the university in the autumn of
1914, just after the outbreak of World War I. Because
she had to work as a babysitter and mother's helper to
earn her room and some money to live on, at first she
did not mingle much with the other students. Day was
also extremely homesick, especially for her little brother
John, fourteen years her junior. Not finding her classes
very interesting, she did not put much time into her stud-
ies. Rather, she spent her time developing as a writer and
reading books she selected for herself. The writers she
chose to read included Jack London; Upton Sinclair; and
the Russians Turgenev, Tolstoy, and her particular favorite, Dostoyevsky. She was drawn to their accounts of the
struggles of the poor and the working class.

This first year of college led her to question the whole
idea of religious faith.

---

[3] Dorothy Day, *The Long Loneliness* (New York: Harper and Brothers,
1952), 38.

It seems to me that I was already shedding it [Christianity] when a professor whom I much admired made a statement in class—I shall always remember it—that religion was something which had brought great comfort to people throughout the ages, so that we ought not to criticize it. I don't remember his exact words, but from the way he spoke of religion the class could infer that the strong were the ones who did not need such props. In my youthful arrogance, in my feeling that I was one of the strong, I felt then for the first time that religion was something that I must ruthlessly cut out of my life.[4]

At this same time Day joined a writers' club on campus, which brought her into contact with the "radical" community at the university and where she made her first friends. Her two best friends from this time were Samson Raphaelson and Rayan Simons. The three spent many hours discussing books and the social issues of the day. Raphaelson was a writer who went on to have great success on Broadway and in Hollywood. Simons came from a wealthy family and was happy to share what she had with Day in a way that never made her feel beholden. Simons was also enthusiastic and encouraging about Day's talent as a writer. Eventually, Simons' radicalism would lead her to work with the communists in China and the Soviet Union. When she died in Moscow in 1927, communists from around the world attended her funeral. Ten years later Day wrote: "And now her [Simons'] dust, in an urn, reposes in Moscow, and I alone pray for her soul, for I am the only one she knew who has a faith in the resurrection of the body and the life everlasting."[5]

Dorothy Day had always felt compassion for the less fortunate people she encountered: the earthquake victims

[4] Day, *Union Square*, 42–43.
[5] Ibid., 55.

of San Francisco and the poor tenement dwellers of Chicago. The readings of Sinclair, London, Tolstoy, and Dostoyevsky had further opened her eyes to the suffering of others. Day recalls: "I was in love now with the masses. I do not remember that I was articulate or reasoned about this love, but it warmed and filled my heart."[6] Filled with the passion of youth, Day joined the Socialist Party. She also came to embrace Karl Marx' motto that religion was merely an opiate of the people meant to help them endure their suffering and to accept the injustices of the capitalist system.

In June 1916 Day's father took a job on a New York paper and moved the family back east. Too emotionally close to her family to endure such a distant separation, Day decided that she was through with school and wanted to work. Day left the university after her sophomore year and never completed a degree. But the return to New York opened up a different life for her.

Journalism and Protest

In 1916, upon her return to New York, Day took a job as a writer for the socialist newspaper the *New York Call*. On her small salary of five dollars a week, she left her parents' home and found a furnished room for herself in the apartment of a Jewish family. Her job led her to explore the situation of the working class in New York and the world of protests and strikes, which were frequent occurrences. She also met and interviewed several important leaders in the various reform movements, including Leon Trotsky, who was to play a leading role in the Russian Revolution.

[6] Day, *Long Loneliness*, 46.

Day herself often joined the picket lines and worked with students active in the peace movement hoping to keep the United States from entering World War I. Many socialists opposed the U.S. entrance into the war because they viewed the conflict as a struggle between imperialist powers who sent out the poor and the working classes of their countries to slaughter each other in the trenches of Europe.

After a few months she left the *Call* and took a job with an influential socialist monthly journal called *The Masses*, whose writing staff included John Reed. (Reed would soon gain fame through his firsthand account of the Russian Revolution, *Ten Days That Shook the World*.) Day's job was to assist with the selection and editing of content for the journal. After the United States entered the war in April 1917, the antiwar stand of the journal led the government to close it and charge its chief editors with inciting rebellion against the government. In November, out of work, Day joined a group of suffragists heading to Washington, D.C., to picket the White House. While Day was not particularly interested in the issue of the women's vote, she was interested in reporting on the government's treatment of the protesters.

Among her group were many women from the upper class of society and from important families, along with the leaders of the suffragist movement. As the group approached the White House, the police arrived, and Day was arrested for the first—but hardly the last—time in her life. The thirty-five women arrested refused bail and were sentenced to thirty days in the prison at Occoquan. They requested to be treated as political prisoners and not as common criminals. This would mean that they could wear their own clothes rather than prison uniforms, receive mail and visitors, and not be required to work. Their request was denied, and they immediately went on a hunger strike to protest their treatment as criminals. The prisoners were then put into solitary confinement. Day wrote about these hours in jail as being "interminably long". Knowing that it would be the only book the guards would allow her, Day asked for a Bible, and on the fourth day she was given one. She took particular comfort in the psalms. But she recalled that this comfort brought with it an inner conflict:

> I clung to the words of comfort in the Bible and as long as the light held out, I read and pondered. Yet all the while I read, my pride was fighting on. I did not want to go to God in defeat and sorrow. I did not want to depend on Him. I was like the child that wants to walk by itself, I kept brushing away the hand that held me up. I tried to persuade myself that I was reading for literary enjoyment. But the words kept echoing in my heart. I prayed and did not know that I prayed.[7]

After ten days, the hunger strike was ended when the pro-testers' demands were met, and they were transferred from the prison to the city jail. On the sixteenth day, president Woodrow Wilson pardoned all of the prisoners, and they were released. Day returned to New York.

Love and Loss

Over the next year Day earned her living as a freelance writer for various left-wing political newspapers and jour-nals. She confessed that she and her friends never really examined the fundamental principles of the schools of Marx, Engels, and Lenin, or of the revolution. As she recalled: "We belonged to that school of youth which

7 Ibid., 81.

lived in the present, lived the life of the senses."[8] She spent
her days writing and her nights drinking in the bars of
Greenwich Village. Day became good friends with the
playwright Eugene O'Neill, who liked to recite Francis Thompson's poem "The Hound of Heaven" as they
sat drinking.

> Gene could recite all of it, and he used to sit there, looking
> dour and black, his head sunk on his chest sighing, "And
> now my heart is as a broken fount wherein tear-drippings
> stagnate." It is one of those poems that awakens the soul,
> recalls to it the fact that God is its destiny. The idea of this
> pursuit fascinated me, the inevitableness of it, the recur-
> rence of it, made me feel that inevitably I would have
> to pause in the mad rush of living to remember my first
> beginning and last end.[9]

Day attempted to hide from her friends how moved she
was by the poem because she felt very strongly that she was
being pursued by God no matter how desperately she tried
to stifle that call. After closing down the bars, Day would
often stop for early morning Mass at Saint Joseph's Church
on Sixth Avenue and kneel in the back. She did not understand what was going on at the altar, but she found warmth
and comfort kneeling with the others.

Day began to feel dissatisfied with the life she was leading. While she still objected to the war, she recognized
that the demand for Red Cross nurses had depleted the
number of nurses available for the hospitals in the city. In
the spring of 1918 Day and her sister, Della, signed on as
nursing students at King's County Hospital in New York.
The work was hard, but Day loved the discipline and the

[8] Ibid., 85.
[9] Day, *Union Square*, 90.

order that nursing required. This was also the time of the influenza epidemic in New York, and Day saw much death and suffering. Since this was a county hospital, most of the patients were the poor, who could not afford any other medical treatment and who often avoided going to the hospital until it was too late.

One day a man who had been beaten up on the docks was brought to the hospital. After he recovered, he stayed on to work as an orderly on Day's ward, and she fell madly in love with him. This man was a journalist and an adventurer named Lionel Moise. Day was not yet twenty-one, and Moise was twenty-nine. In her autobiographical writings, Day avoided talking about this time of her life because she did not want to write about those with whom she was "intimately associated".[10] What we do know about this relationship comes to us mainly from her novel, *The Eleventh Virgin*, which was published in 1924. The character of June in the novel is obviously Dorothy Day. After her conversion, ashamed and embarrassed at the revelations in the novel, Day tracked down and destroyed copies of the book. But toward the end of her life, when William D. Miller began to write her biography, she handed him a copy with the acknowledgment "It's all true."[11]

From the novel, we learn that Day left her job in the hospital to live with Moise. Her description of their relationship is one of passion in which she was dominated by her love for Moise and by his controlling jealousy. Though Day wanted to marry him, Moise always reminded her that this was a casual affair and that he had no intentions of marrying her. "None of his plans for the future included

[10] Day, *Long Loneliness*, 94.
[11] William D. Miller, *Dorothy Day: A Biography* (San Francisco: Harper and Row, 1982), xiii.

her."[12] In the summer of 1919, after they had been together for about a year, Day became pregnant. She knew that Moise did not want to have a child and that he would leave her "as soon as she began to show".[13] Though Day wanted the child, through the character of June she told how

> she could not sacrifice her pride and go to a home to have a baby. She could sacrifice every vestige of pride—throw it all into the flames to keep her love burning. Her love for a man. But not her love for the child that was beginning to form in her. She could not go to her mother for either help or sympathy.... The same pride kept her from doing that.[14]

After four months she told Moise she was pregnant, and they agreed she would get an abortion. She went to the apartment of an abortionist, and there her child was killed. Moise had told her he would pick her up afterward, but he never appeared. Finally, ashamed of what the abortionist would think, she took a taxi to her apartment and found a note from Moise telling her he had hopped a ship to Venezuela. In the novel the note reveals Moise's justification for running out on her:

> After all, you are only one of God knows how many millions of women who go through the same thing, and why I should so far forget myself as to suffer the commonplace emotions of a man who is about to become a father, I don't see. It is entirely against my principles and you would not respect me if I did not live up to my principles.[15]

[12] Dorothy Day, *The Eleventh Virgin* (New York: Albert and Charles Boni, 1924), 295.
[13] Ibid., 299.
[14] Ibid., 299–300.
[15] Ibid., 309.

Day was devastated by her abortion and the end of her relationship with Moise. She even attempted suicide. For Day, the abortion was the great tragedy of her life.[16] In a diary entry more than fifty years later, Day revealed that she still felt guilty about her sins from this time of her life, specifically the abortion.[17] In a letter Day wrote to a young woman in 1973, Day shared this: "I'm praying very hard for you this morning, because I myself have been through much of what you have been through. Twice I tried to take my own life, and the dear Lord pulled me thru [sic] that darkness—I was rescued from that darkness. My sickness was physical too, since I had had an abortion with bad after-effects, and in a way my sickness of mind was a penance I had to endure."[18]

The End of Youth

Humiliated and distraught, a few months later in the spring of 1920, Day met and married a man named Barkeley Tobey. He had family money and worked in the publishing business. Tobey was sixteen years older than Day, and this was his fourth marriage. That summer they left to spend a year touring Europe, visiting England, France, and Italy. It was during this period that Day wrote *The Eleventh Virgin*. By the time they returned to New York in the

[16] See Jim Forest, "Servant of God Dorothy Day", Catholic Worker Movement website, http://www.catholicworker.org/dorothyday/servantofgod. Cf. Jim Forest, *All Is Grace: A Biography of Dorothy Day* (Maryknoll, N.Y.: Orbis Books, 2012), 326.

[17] Dorothy Day, diary entry, December 24, 1976, in *The Duty of Delight: The Diaries of Dorothy Day*, ed. Robert Ellsberg (Milwaukee, Wis.: Marquette University Press, 2008), 272.

[18] Dorothy Day to a Young Woman in Distress, February 6, 1973, in *All the Way to Heaven: The Selected Letters of Dorothy Day*, ed. Robert Ellsberg (Milwaukee, Wis.: Marquette University Press, 2010), 397.

summer of 1921, the marriage was over. She left Tobey to go to Chicago, where Moise was now living, with the hope of reconciling with him.

While in Chicago, Day was in contact with Moise; and while she saw him socially, she was not able to reignite a relationship with him. During this time she befriended a woman named Mae Cramer, who was also in love with Moise. Cramer's own desperation over Moise led her to attempt suicide by a drug overdose. When she was released from the hospital, Day took care of her. The two women found a room at a boardinghouse run by the labor organization the Industrial Workers of the World (IWW), or the "Wobblies". Because of the group's radical socialist political views, the Wobblies were subject to government surveillance. The first night that Day and Cramer stayed at the house, it was raided by the police. As the only women in the house, Day and Cramer were arrested and charged with prostitution.

This trip to jail was quite different from her experience in Washington, D.C., when she was arrested with the suffragists, most of whom were upper-class society women. This time Day was jailed in a crowded cell with women who were drug addicts and prostitutes. She was touched by the way the other women tried to help her. She could also see the extent to which their circumstances in life had contributed to their bad decisions. For Day, "to see human beings racked, by their own will, made one feel the depth of the disorder of the world."[19] She felt the "sadness of sin" but also anger with a system that did not provide better alternatives for these poor women. After three or four days, through the intervention of a journalist friend, Day and Cramer were released from jail, and the prostitution charges were dropped.

[19] Day, *Long Loneliness*, 104.

In her accounts of this time in her life, Day often referred to how her encounters with religious people, either in her daily experience or in the books she was reading, impressed her. In particular, she was drawn to the way in which they confronted moral problems with firm principles. From the young women praying in the house where she rented a room, to Dostoyevsky's Sonya reading the Gospel in *Crime and Punishment*, Day was moved by the nobility of people who were religious. And Day began to see that "worship, adoration, thanksgiving, supplication— these were the noblest acts of which men were capable in this life."[20]

Soon Day left Chicago and took a job on a newspaper in New Orleans. While there, she pursued her growing interest in religion. Day felt Catholicism to be something "rich and real and fascinating" but also felt outside of it. She lived near the cathedral and one evening went to Benediction. Day remembered: "It was the first time I had been present at Benediction and it made a profound impression on me. The very physical attitude of devotion of those about me made me bow my head. But did I feel the Presence there? I do not know."[21] Day began to feel drawn to Catholicism and bought a book of Catholic prayers. A friend of hers, a Russian Jew, bought Day her first rosary, and she began to pray with it.

In the spring of 1924 a movie studio bought the rights to *The Eleventh Virgin*. While no movie was ever made of the novel, Day received the sum of $2,500. Suddenly "rich", Day returned to New York and bought for herself a small beach house on Staten Island, a change that would mark the beginning of the next chapters of her life.

---

[20] Ibid., 107.
[21] Day, *Union Square*, 112–13.

Chapter Two

A NEW LIFE AND CONVERSION

Natural Happiness

Upon her return to New York in 1924, Dorothy Day resumed many of the old friendships she had there. She joined a circle of writers and bohemians that included the poet Hart Crane, the novelist John Dos Passos, the critic Kenneth Burke, and the editor and writer Malcolm Cowley. Cowley's wife, Peggy, convinced Day that she should buy a place on Staten Island so that she would have the time and the solitude necessary for her writing. The two traveled out to the west end of the island, where Day found a small fisherman's cabin that suited her needs perfectly. Day loved living on the water. She took long walks along the beach, stopping to visit with her many neighbors. She remembered it as a time of great joy and peace: "It was a peace, curiously enough, divided against itself. I was happy but my very happiness made me know that there was a greater happiness to be obtained from life than any I had ever known. . . . I began consciously to pray more."[1] Day developed the habit of praying as she walked on the beach or into the nearby town on her errands. She would carry

[1] Dorothy Day, *The Long Loneliness* (New York: Harper and Brothers, 1952), 116.

the rosary her friend had given her in New Orleans. But she was still haunted by the idea, which she had encountered in Marx, that "religion is the opiate of the people" and that her praying was a way to ease her pain.

> "But," I reasoned with myself, "I am praying because I am happy, not because I am unhappy. I did not turn to God in unhappiness, in grief, in despair—to get consolation, to get something from Him."
> And encouraged that I was praying because I wanted to thank Him, I went on praying.[2]

At this time Day also began to attend Mass regularly on Sunday mornings.

Among Day's friends at this time was Kenneth Burke's wife, Lily, who introduced Day to her brother, Forster Batterham, a self-proclaimed anarchist. Soon Day and Batterham fell in love. He was from North Carolina, raised as an only son with seven sisters. By 1925 Day and Batterham had entered into what Day described as a "common-law marriage". Batterham worked in the city and on the weekends went out to Staten Island to live with Day.

Batterham was a naturalist who fished, explored the beach, and at night studied the stars. Day described how on their walks they would collect and study the things they would find on the beach. Dorothy credited him with opening up a whole new world for her and giving her a deep appreciation of the beauty of nature. In the evenings they would read books together or Forster would read to her from the newspapers. Initially this relationship brought her great happiness, and from her writings it is clear that she loved him deeply.

---

[2] Ibid., 132–33.

I loved him in every way, as a wife, as a mother even. I loved him for all he knew and pitied him for all he didn't know. I loved him for the odds and ends I had to fish out of his sweater pockets and for the sand and shells he brought in with his fishing. I loved his lean cold body as he got into bed smelling of the sea, and loved his integrity and stubborn pride.[3]

But Batterham did not share Day's growing interest in faith. As an anarchist he rejected all religious institutions; as a materialist he rejected anything supernatural. Day found it ironic that the deepening love of nature that Batterham was fostering in her was at the same time bringing her closer to God. He wondered why she could not just be satisfied with the beauty of nature without bringing God into the picture, while Day wondered why he could not see how this same beauty pointed to the necessity of God.

In June 1925 Day realized she was pregnant. Ever since her abortion five years earlier, she had feared that her womb had been damaged and that she would be unable to have children.[4] Finding she was pregnant again gave Day a "blissful joy". God was giving her a second chance at motherhood, and she was determined not to reject His wonderful gift this time. One of Day's biographers, William Miller, described Day's reaction: "She felt now that some disease of her soul had been cured, that God had forgiven her, that a pall that hung over her had been removed."[5]

Batterham did not share Day's enthusiasm, and his response to her pregnancy dampened her happiness. Because

[3] Ibid., 148.

[4] Jim Forest, *Love Is the Measure: A Biography of Dorothy Day* (Maryknoll, N.Y.: Orbis Books, 1986), 46.

[5] William D. Miller, *Dorothy Day: A Biography* (San Francisco: Harper and Row, 1982), 179.

he prided himself on being an individualist, he could not see himself as a father with responsibilities. Further, while he loved nature, he saw the world of men as one of violence and injustice. Thus, he did not think it was right to bring a child into this world. Finally, he feared that a child might come between him and Day. But Day was determined that this time nothing would prevent her from giving birth to her child.

Motherhood and Conversion

As Day neared the end of her pregnancy, she moved to an apartment in New York City, where her sister could help her through the days prior to delivery and the first weeks of motherhood. On March 4, 1926, Tamar Teresa was born. Day chose the Hebrew name Tamar, which means "little palm tree", because a close friend who was Jewish had a daughter by that name and Day thought it was lovely. She chose Teresa after Saint Teresa of Avila, whom she had read about and admired. Day was determined to have her daughter baptized in the Catholic Church even though she knew this would create difficulties with Batterham. Day explained: "I knew that I was not going to have her floundering through many years as I had done, doubting and hesitating, undisciplined and amoral. I felt it was the greatest thing I could do for my child. For myself, I prayed for the gift of faith. I was sure yet not sure."[6]

After six weeks in the city, Day returned to the beach house. She loved being a mother. Although at the end of the day she would be exhausted, she found herself in a "stupor of contentment". But her joy was also mixed with sadness because she knew that the decision to have

[6]Day, *Long Loneliness*, 136.

Tamar baptized would cause an irreconcilable split with Batterham. And so for a while she put off the christening. Finally, Day knew that she could not delay her decision anymore and that Tamar must receive the sacrament of baptism. But she knew very few Catholics and had no idea how to go about it. One day she saw a nun walking down the road and approached her to ask how she could have Tamar baptized. Sister Aloysia, a member of the Sisters of Charity, did not seem at all surprised that a young mother would ask her this question and was very matter-of-fact about how this could be done. Day liked her immediately. The old nun also understood the difficulties Day faced when Day explained her situation with Batterham, and she was prepared to support her through it. Day recalled:

> She took me under her protection immediately. She did not make little of my difficulties, nor did she think for a minute that they were insurmountable. There was a hard row to hoe in front of us, was her attitude, but we would get through it. She would hang on to that long, formidable-looking rosary of hers, hang on to it like an anchor, and together we would ride out the gale of opposition and controversy. All we had to do was depend on prayer.[7]

Sister Aloysia taught Day the catechism and gave her material to read in preparation for Tamar's baptism, which took place in July. But Sister Aloysia also kept asking Day how she could raise her daughter Catholic if she was not Catholic herself and admonished her to join the Church. Day knew that the sister was right, and she recognized that the Church was the home she had been seeking for so long.

---

[7] Dorothy Day, *From Union Square to Rome* (Maryknoll, N.Y.: Orbis Books, 2006), 139.

Day clearly understood that because Forster would never consent to any marriage ceremony, her decision to enter the Church would mean the end of her relationship with him. She knew that she could not become Catholic and at the same time reject the teachings of the Church on love and family by continuing to live in sin with a man, no matter how deeply she loved him. Day understood that while entering the Church was a free choice, it brought with it the responsibility of obedience. In *The Long Loneliness* she wrote: "There was the legislation of the Church in regard to marriage, a stumbling block to many. That was where I began to be troubled, to be afraid. To become a Catholic meant for me to give up a mate with whom I was much in love. It got to the point where it was the simple question of whether I chose God or man."[8] Day appreciated the fact that it was through her love of Forster, both spiritual and physical, that she had come to understand what love was, and she was grateful for this. But with the birth of her child she also became aware that "the final object of this love and gratitude was God." And since it was becoming clear to Day that the Catholic Church was the one true Church, established by Christ, she could not claim to love God while ignoring Church teaching.

Day had no illusion about what she would have to give up when she converted. God was giving her the chance to prove the love that she claimed she felt for Him. But she did not enter the Church immediately. On the advice of a priest who understood the importance of Tamar having a father and Day a husband, she tried for over a year to work things out with Batterham. Day was also troubled with the thought that by joining the Church she was somehow turning her back on the issues of social justice that continued to be the focus of her thought and writing.

[8] Day, *Long Loneliness*, 140.

At this time she was still unaware of the Church's teachings on these issues.

Though he initially claimed not to want to be a father, Forster took great interest and delight in Tamar. And Day knew that this would make their final split even more difficult for everyone. This year of waiting was marked by increasing tension between Day and Batterham over religion, several times resulting in his moving out. And then came the final parting. Day recalled: "By winter [1927] the tension had become so great that an explosion occurred and we separated again. When he returned, as he always had, I would not let him in the house; my heart was breaking with my own determination to make an end, once and for all, to the torture we were undergoing."[9] The next day she was baptized—conditionally, because she had already been baptized in the Episcopal church. She made her first confession right afterward and received her first Communion the next morning. Day had taken the decisive step: "I was a Catholic at last though at that moment I never felt less the joy and peace and consolation which I know from my own experience religion can bring."[10] The final step of this part of her journey had not been easy. But a year later, upon her confirmation, all feelings of uncertainty finally left her. She recalled this as a joyous occasion. Day took the confirmation name Maria Teresa.

Single Mother

After her separation from Batterham, Day was faced with the task of supporting herself and Tamar. She continued with her writing and made some money selling her short

[9] Ibid., 148.
[10] Day, *Union Square*, 146.

stories. She also got a job working for Metro-Goldwyn-
Mayer (MGM) writing synopses of novels at six dollars a
novel, and for a time she worked as a cook at the Marist
novitiate on the island. Her letters to Batterham reflect her
continued love for him and are filled with pleas for him
to marry her so they could live as a family. A typical letter
from 1929, written to Batterham in New York while Day
was visiting her mother in Florida, revealed her love and
her loneliness:

> I have felt nothing but blank loneliness since I left you.
> Life is indeed a most miserable affair. Why don't you
> become reasonable or indulgent or whatever you want to
> call it and tell me to come back and marry you? We could
> be so happy together. And even if we fought it would be
> better than this blank dead feeling. You know I love you
> and it isn't just loneliness which makes me long for you.[11]

In other letters she assures Batterham that she will not
try to impose her religion on him and asks only that she
be allowed to practice her faith and raise Tamar (and any
future children) within the Church.

In August 1929 Day received an offer from Pathé
Motion Picture Company in Hollywood to become a
dialogue writer. She had sent them a play she had written, and they were impressed enough to offer her a three-
month salary at $125 a week. So Day packed up Tamar
and moved to California. But Day found life in California
lonely, since most of her work involved sitting by herself in an office, where she made few friends. She also
thought the movies she was asked to work on were silly

---

[11] Dorothy Day to Forster Batterham, September 10, 1929, in *All the Way
to Heaven: The Selected Letters of Dorothy Day*, ed. Robert Ellsberg (Milwaukee,
Wis.: Marquette University Press, 2010), 27.

and trivial. During her time in California the stock market crashed, in October 1929, marking the beginning of the Great Depression. After the three months, when her contract was not renewed, Day considered returning to New York, but she feared that this would be an occasion for sin because she still "hungered too much to return to Forster".[12] Instead, Day bought a car, took what money she had saved, and moved with Tamar to Mexico City, where it was cheaper to live.

Day enjoyed her time in Mexico, and it was her first experience of living in a Catholic culture. She made some money by writing articles for the Catholic journal *Commonweal*.[13] One of these articles tells of a trip to the shrine of Our Lady of Guadalupe. But after six months in Mexico Tamar contracted malaria, and she and Day returned to the United States in the spring of 1930. Day settled in New York, where she continued to make a living writing for newspapers and journals. But she was becoming increasingly concerned about the crisis of the poor and the homeless and felt that while her radical friends were taking direct action in these matters, she as a Catholic was doing nothing, and the Church, to her knowledge, was offering little leadership. She began to attend daily Mass and weekly Benediction and returned to the writings of Saint Teresa of Avila.

In November 1932 Day was hired by the Jesuit magazine *America* to report on the Hunger March in Washington, D.C. The Hunger March was organized in New York by the communist Unemployed Council; similar groups around the country also went to the nation's capital to

---

[12] Day, *Long Loneliness*, 158.
[13] Several of these essays have been collected in *Dorothy Day: Writings from "Commonweal"*, ed. Patrick Jordan (Collegeville, Minn.: Liturgical Press, 2002).

protest the conditions of the unemployed. They demanded jobs, pensions, and help for mothers and children. In New York about six hundred protesters gathered and left for Washington, D.C., in a caravan of old cars and moving vans. Day left Tamar with her brother John and his wife, Tessa, with whom she had been sharing an apartment. She and her friend and fellow journalist Mary Heaton Vorse made their way to Washington by bus.

The popular press portrayed the protest as a communist attempt to seize the capital, and the caravan was met with hostility along the way. In Wilmington, Delaware, where the protesters from New York had stopped for the night at a Protestant church, the police threw tear gas in the windows and clubbed and arrested their leaders. Still, the groups proceeded to Washington, but when they arrived, police barricades blocked the highway and prevented them from entering the city. The protesters camped out in the cold for three days, until on December 8, the Feast of the Immaculate Conception, the police took down the barricades, and the three thousand protesters from around the country were allowed to enter the city. Day and Vorse had taken a cheap room on Massachusetts Avenue and were present to watch the protesters march down the streets of the capital.

Day found the protesters very moving. She recalled the conflict she felt in her own heart as she watched the communists march past:

> I stood on the curb and watched them, joy and pride in the courage of this band of men and women mounting in my heart, and with it a bitterness too that since I was now a Catholic, with fundamental philosophical differences, I could not be out there with them. I could write, I could protest, to arouse the conscience, but where was the Catholic leadership in the gathering of bands of men and women together, for the actual works of mercy that

the comrades had always made part of their technique in reaching the workers?

How little, how puny my work had been since becoming a Catholic, I thought. How self-centered, how ingrown, how lacking in sense of community! My summer of quiet reading and prayer, my self-absorption seemed sinful as I watched my brothers in their struggle, not for themselves but for others. How our dear Lord must love them, I kept thinking to myself. They were His friends, His comrades, and who knows how close to His heart in their attempts to work for justice.[14]

After finishing her article on the protest, Day went that evening to the National Shrine of the Immaculate Conception on the campus of the Catholic University of America to attend Mass on this Feast of the Immaculate Conception. The upper church was still under construction, so she went to the crypt church. Day recalled: "There I offered up a special prayer, a prayer which came with tears and with anguish, that some way would open up for me to use what talents I possessed for my fellow workers, for the poor."[15] She did not have to wait long for her prayer to be answered.

Peter Maurin

When Day returned to New York the next day, eager to see Tamar, she found a fifty-five-year-old Frenchman with calloused hands and a weather-beaten face waiting in her apartment. Wearing a shabby suit, the man was talking with her sister-in-law, Tessa. He introduced himself as Peter Maurin and explained that he had been given

[14] Day, *Long Loneliness*, 165.
[15] Ibid., 166.

her address by the editor of *Commonweal*. He immediately began talking to Day about working with him to serve the poor and to put the message of the Gospels into action. Day was surprised; it was not until later that she realized that through this man's spirit and ideas God would answer her prayer, would give direction to the rest of her life.

In later years Day was always quick to acknowledge the profound effect Peter Maurin had on her life. "Without him, I would never have been able to find a way of working that would have satisfied my conscience. Maurin's arrival changed everything. I finally found a purpose in my life and the teacher I needed."[16] While Day had fully embraced the Church in her conversion, she had not been exposed to the Church's rich history of philosophy and theology. Peter Maurin became her teacher in this area and provided Day with an understanding of the Church's teachings, particularly on social issues, which allowed her to join together her faith and her strong desire to serve others.

When Maurin tracked Day down in December 1932, he was looking for someone to help him promote a social program grounded in the Gospels and the teachings of the Catholic Church. In particular, he was drawn to Day as a journalist who could help him found a newspaper for spreading his ideas. He had been impressed by her writings in *Commonweal* and *America*. Day feared that Maurin had an exaggerated sense of her abilities.

Day came to see that Maurin's religious and social convictions ran as deeply as her own. Together they went on to create what came to be known as the Catholic Worker movement, which some have identified as the

---

[16] Dorothy Day, *Peter Maurin: Apostle to the World*, with Francis J. Sicius (Maryknoll, N.Y.: Orbis Books, 2004), xxvii.

most influential Catholic lay movement in America in the twentieth century. Day always emphasized Maurin's role in its founding:

> Peter Maurin is most truly the founder of the Catholic Worker movement. I would never have had an idea in my head about such work if it had not been for him. I was a journalist, I loved to write, but was far better at making criticism of the social order than offering any constructive ideas in relation to it. Peter had a program, [and] I tried to follow it.... He opened our minds to great horizons, he gave us a vision.[17]

Pierre Joseph Orestide Maurin was born on May 8, 1877, in the small town of Oultet in the Languedoc region of southeastern France. His mother died when he was seven, after having given birth to five children. Two years later his father remarried, and his second wife bore him nineteen children. Peter Maurin grew up in this large peasant family that lived off the land, and his earliest experiences were of community, sharing, and support. When Maurin was sixteen he entered the novitiate of the Christian Brothers and continued his education. He remained with them for nine years but never took final vows.

After he left the Christian Brothers in 1902, Maurin became active in an influential Catholic social movement called le Sillon (the Furrow). Founded by Marc Sangier, it promoted the study of history, politics, and economics in light of Christian values. When le Sillon took a more secular turn, Maurin left the group. In 1909 he and a friend sailed to America to pursue homesteading in Saskatchewan, Canada. After two years of this difficult life,

[17] Dorothy Day to Brendan O'Grady, June 2, 1954, quoted in Day, *Peter Maurin*, xvii.

his friend died, and Maurin abandoned the project. He took jobs across both Canada and the United States, laying railroad track, logging, laying brick, and working in coal mines and steel mills. During this time he also continued to read and to study, particularly philosophy, the teachings of the Church, and the lives of the saints. He settled for a while in Chicago and worked as a French tutor. By the mid-1920s Maurin had taken a position as a handyman in a Catholic boys' school in upstate New York, and he would frequently travel into New York City to use the libraries and discuss his ideas with whoever would listen to him. Through years of hard work, study, prayer, and reflection, he developed a theory of Christian life, which he was eager to promote and actualize. At the age of fifty-five, Peter Maurin came to ask Dorothy Day to collaborate with him in this work, and with her help he was able to put this theory into practice as the foundation of the Catholic Worker movement.

Day and Maurin would work together for the next seventeen years, until his death in May 1949. Through Day's writings and actions Maurin's ideas continued to live and flourish.

Chapter Three

THE INTELLECTUAL
FOUNDATIONS OF THE
CATHOLIC WORKER

Important theological and philosophical ideas shaped the
thinking of Dorothy Day and Peter Maurin as they established the Catholic Worker movement. In addition to
several papal encyclicals, Maurin had studied the Catholic
philosophical tradition and followed contemporary devel-
opments in philosophy, particularly the movement called
French personalism. He was eager to share these ideas with
Day, and they came to influence her thought and writing.

Rerum Novarum and *Quadragesimo Anno*

Peter Maurin's philosophy grew out of an attempt to find
an alternative to the two social and economic systems
that dominated the thinking of his day: communism and
capitalism. He believed that Catholic philosophy and the
teachings of the Catholic Church offered that alternative.
Maurin was convinced that both communism and capitalism failed to promote a society in which men can realize a
truly human life. He often summarized his goal as building
a society in which it was easier for people to be good.

Capitalism can be defined as an economic system based upon the private ownership of the means by which people make a living. That is to say that private individuals own factories, farms, companies, and so forth. At the heart of this system is the belief that when individuals are responsible for themselves and are free to pursue their own self-interest, the society as a whole benefits. For example, if a person works hard and saves his money and opens a business, he is able to provide for himself and his family and to increase his own wealth. In pursuing this self-interest, he also creates jobs for others who work at his business and spends his money to support other businesses. So his pursuit of his own wealth and security improves the condition of those around him. In a capitalist system the free market determines the production and distribution of goods and services.

Communism, on the other hand, does not treat persons as individuals but emphasizes people as parts of a collective. It is critical of capitalism for creating a conflict between two classes: the owners (the bourgeoisie) and the workers (the proletariat). Because owners in a capitalist system are motivated by the increase in profits and the accumulation of wealth, they tend to pay workers the lowest wages possible to keep down their costs and to get the most work out of the fewest workers, regardless of the toll on the worker. Communism eliminates private ownership and places the means of production in the hands of a strong centralized state that distributes the wealth to provide for all the citizens, and thus eliminates the distinction between the classes. The state determines the production and distribution of goods and services, not the free market. Communism maintains that individual freedom must be subordinated to the collective good.

Peter Maurin believed that Catholic thought, grounded in the Gospels, offered a third way of thinking about society that avoided the dangers entailed in both capitalism and communism. He shared his vision with Day and introduced her to the Church teachings and encyclicals that address questions of social and economic justice. Maurin embraced the views found in Pope Leo XIII's encyclical letter on the condition of the working class, *Rerum Novarum*, which appeared in 1891, and which were reaffirmed and expanded in Pope Pius XI's encyclical letter on the reconstruction of the social order, *Quadragesimo Anno*, which was promulgated forty years later in 1931. In his letter, Pius XI called people to avoid the misunderstandings of the human person that are at work in both communism and capitalism.

> Accordingly, twin rocks of shipwreck must be carefully avoided. For, as one is wrecked upon, or comes close to, what is known as "individualism" by denying or minimizing the social and public character of the right of property, so by rejecting or minimizing the private and individual character of this same right, one inevitably runs into "collectivism" or at least closely approaches its tenets.[1]

As the Church rejects the modern notion that we are all isolated individuals pursuing only our own self-interest, so also it rejects the idea that we are merely members of a collective with few individual rights.

In *Rerum Novarum* Leo XIII pointed out the errors he saw as inherent in both communism and capitalism. For example, with regard to communism, the Pope reasserted the Church's teaching that God intended man to own private property that he earned through his labors because he has a responsibility to meet the needs of his family.

---

[1] Pius XI, *Quadragesimo Anno* (1931), no. 46.

Thus, the wholesale transfer of goods from individuals to the community at large would be an injustice.[2]

> The socialists, working on the poor man's envy of the rich, are striving to do away with private property, and contend that individual possessions should become the common property of all, to be administered by the State or by municipal bodies. They hold that by thus transferring property from private individuals to the community, the present mischievous state of things will be set to rights, inasmuch as each citizen will then get his fair share of whatever there is to enjoy. But their contentions are so clearly powerless to end the controversy that were they carried into effect the working man himself would be among the first to suffer. They are, moreover, emphatically unjust, for they would rob the lawful possessor, distort the functions of the State, and create utter confusion in the community.[3]

Further, contrary to Marx' call in the *Communist Manifesto* for the "abolition of all right of inheritance",[4] the Pope asserted that parents have a right to pass on their property to their children.[5] He was critical of Marx' call for "a heavy progressive or graduated income tax",[6] which would excessively tax the wealthy in order to redistribute wealth:

> The right to possess private property is derived from nature, not from man; and the State has the right to

---

[2] See Leo XIII, *Rerum Novarum* (1891), nos. 4–11.

[3] Ibid., no. 4.

[4] Karl Marx and Friedrich Engels, *Manifesto of the Communist Party*, in *The Marx-Engels Reader*, ed. Robert Tucker, 2nd ed. (New York: W. W. Norton, 1978), 490.

[5] Leo XIII, *Rerum Novarum*, no. 13.

[6] Marx and Engels, *Manifesto*, 490.

control its use in the interests of the public good alone,
but by no means to absorb it altogether. The State would
therefore be unjust and cruel if under the name of taxation
it were to deprive the private owner of more than is fair.[7]

And of course the Holy Father was quick to condemn
any system, including Marxism, that fails to recognize that
human needs are not merely material but also moral and
spiritual.

On the other hand, Leo XIII also made strong criticisms
of capitalism. While he recognized the rights of property
ownership, he also recognized that once one's own needs
have been met, "it becomes a duty to give to the indigent
out of what remains over."[8] The right to private property is
not absolute and is subordinate to the principle of the universal destination of goods, because the goods of creation
are intended for everyone.[9] Property has a social character
in that God created the world for the good of all, not just
the good of a few, and therefore one has a responsibility
to provide for the entire family of mankind. In *Quadragesimo Anno*, Pius XI reiterated this teaching: "A person's
superfluous income, that is, income which he does not
need to sustain life fittingly and with dignity, is not left
wholly to his own free determination. Rather the Sacred
Scriptures and Fathers of the Church constantly declare
in the most explicit language that the rich are bound by
a very grave precept to practice almsgiving, beneficence,
and munificence."[10]

[7] Leo XIII, *Rerum Novarum*, no. 47.

[8] Ibid., no. 22.

[9] Pontifical Council for Justice and Peace, *Compendium of the Social Doctrine
of the Church* (Washington, D.C.: United States Conference of Catholic Bishops, 2005), no. 177.

[10] Pius XI, *Quadragesimo Anno* (1931), no. 50.

Further, in *Rerum Novarum* Leo XIII condemned practices that exploit workers and distort work from something
that ennobles man to something that degrades him:

> The following duties bind the wealthy owner and the
> employer: not to look upon their work people as their
> bondsmen, but to respect in every man his dignity as a per-
> son ennobled by Christian character. They are reminded
> that according to natural reason and Christian philosophy,
> working for gain is creditable, not shameful, to a man,
> since it enables him to earn an honorable livelihood; but
> to misuse men as though they were things in the pursuit
> of gain, or to value them solely for their physical powers—
> that is truly shameful and inhuman.[11]

The Holy Father also recognized that the employer has an
obligation to pay a just wage to workers:

> Let the working man and the employer make free agree-
> ments, and in particular let them agree freely as to the
> wages; nevertheless, there underlies a dictate of natu-
> ral justice more imperious and ancient than any bargain
> between man and man, namely, that wages ought not to
> be insufficient to support a frugal and well-behaved wage-
> earner. If through necessity or fear of a worse evil the
> workman accept harder conditions because an employer
> or contractor will afford him no better, he is made the
> victim of force and injustice.[12]

Similarly, Pius XI maintained:

> In the first place, the worker must be paid a wage suf-
> ficient to support him and his family.... Mothers, con-
> centrating on household duties, should work primarily in

---

[11] Leo XIII, *Rerum Novarum*, no. 20.
[12] Ibid., no. 45.

the home or in it's immediate vicinity. It is an intolerable abuse, and to be abolished at all costs, for mothers on account of the father's low wage to be forced to engage in gainful occupations outside the home to the neglect of their proper cares and duties, especially the training of children. Every effort must therefore be made that fathers of families receive a wage large enough to meet ordinary family needs adequately.[13]

Both Popes argued that workers have a right to form organizations and unions in order to protect their rights and improve their conditions.[14]

Finally, since Pius XI wrote *Quadragesimo Anno* against the backdrop of the Great Depression, which was in part the result of the collapse of the financial markets, he had strong words for those who do not labor but only use money to make money:

> In the first place, it is obvious that not only is wealth concentrated in our times but an immense power and despotic economic dictatorship is consolidated in the hands of a few, who often are not owners but only the trustees and managing directors of invested funds which they administer according to their own arbitrary will and pleasure.
>
> This dictatorship is being most forcibly exercised by those who, since they hold the money and completely control it, control credit also and rule the lending of money. Hence they regulate the flow, so to speak, of the life-blood whereby the entire economic system lives, and have so firmly in their grasp the soul, as it were, of economic life that no one can breathe against their will.
>
> This concentration of power and might, the characteristic mark, as it were, of contemporary economic life, is the fruit that the unlimited freedom of struggle among

[13] Pius XI, *Quadragesimo Anno*, no. 71.
[14] Leo XIII, *Rerum Novarum*, no. 49; Pius XI, *Quadragesimo Anno*, no. 87.

competitors has of its own nature produced, and which
lets only the strongest survive; and this is often the same as
saying, those who fight the most violently, those who give
least heed to their conscience.[15]

Both Leo XIII and Pius XI emphasized the need for an
economic system that recognizes the inherent dignity of
all persons. Along with these encyclicals and other Church
documents articulating the Catholic tradition, Peter Maurin and Dorothy Day were also influenced by the the-
ories of several Catholic philosophers. Four of the most
important ideas that were central to their understanding of
the Catholic Worker are personalism, the common good,
subsidiarity, and distributism.

Personalism

Personalism offers a view of the human person that avoids
the overemphasis on the individual and individual freedom found in capitalism but does not accept communism's
emphasis on the collective or state at the expense of the
individual person. Personalism is an idea that explicitly
emerged in the late nineteenth century but has its roots
in traditional Christian thinking. Maurin was particularly
influenced by the development of this idea in two French
philosophers who were his contemporaries: Jacques Maritain (1882–1973) and Emmanuel Mounier (1905–1950).
These French personalists maintained that Western civ-
ilization was in crisis and that this was not primarily an
economic or a political crisis but rather a spiritual crisis that
demanded a spiritual response. The heart of personalism is

---

[15] Pius XI, *Quadragesimo Anno*, nos. 105–7.

the emphasis on the absolute value of every human person. This value is not derived from what this person produces or possesses, as capitalism tends to presume, nor does it derive from his role as part of a collective, as communism presumes. Rather, the value of each individual comes from his very existence as a human being made in the image and likeness of God. In particular, personalism emphasizes the dignity that freedom bestows upon the person, allowing him to participate in perfecting this image through choosing to follow the teachings of the Gospels.

Personalism rejects the view of human freedom that has come to dominate the modern world, the mistaken view that freedom means being liberated from any limits on one's choices in life, the view that a free person is one who spontaneously follows any impulse without constraint. On the contrary, Mounier described freedom as not mere spontaneity but a response to a call in a particular situation that demands human action.[16] As such, freedom brings with it a personal responsibility for answering that call in a particular historical situation, and true human freedom is to choose the means that will realize one's vocation. But this realization requires the context of a community that provides the material and spiritual conditions necessary for persons to answer this call. According to Mounier: "One does not free man by detaching him from the bonds that paralyze him; one frees man by attaching him to his destiny."[17] For the personalists, this destiny is ultimately salvation.

Personalism also emphasizes the understanding of the human being as an embodied soul. Embodiment always places the person in a particular historical situation, which

---

[16] Emmanuel Mounier, *Personalism*, trans. Philip Mairet (Notre Dame, Ind.: University of Notre Dame Press, 1970), 61.

[17] Emmanuel Mounier, *Révolution personaliste et communautaire*, in *Œuvres*, vol. 1, *1931–1939* (Paris: Éditions du Seuil, 1961), 212. My translation.

again means that one is not merely an individual, as capitalism may presume, but always part of a particular community, in relationship to others. The person's spiritual
aspect, on the other hand, demands recognition that one
has needs beyond the material, which no economic system can satisfy, contrary to the false hopes of communism.
Thus, it is impossible to understand the person apart from
community or to reduce the person to a purely material
being. For the personalists, the ultimate foundation of the
human community is that we all share the same vocation
in that we are all called to union with God. We are also
united by the fact that the truth is the same for all. Thus,
thinking that denies our vocation from God or replaces
truth with relativism destroys the possibility of community. Finally, for the personalist the model for understanding the human community is the Trinity, where we find
three Persons in one God. Like the divine Persons, human
persons, though distinct from each other, are always united
with each other in a community.

The Common Good

Our communal nature is best understood in terms of our
common orientation to what the tradition calls "the common good". As Peter Maurin observed: "Man is more than
an individual with individual rights; he is a person with personal duties toward God, himself and his fellow man. As a
person man cannot serve God without serving the Common
Good."[18] The idea of the common good, which has always
been a foundational principle of Catholic social teaching,
became a central tenant of the Catholic Worker movement. Recognizing the dignity of each person as a central
truth, the Church defines the common good as "the sum of

[18] Peter Maurin, *Easy Essays* (Chicago: Franciscan Herald, 1977), 44.

those conditions of social life which allow social groups and individual members relatively thorough and ready access to their own fulfillment".[19] Since humans are by nature social beings, "they are not able to achieve their full development by themselves for living a truly human life."[20]

Jacques Maritain describes the common good this way: "It is the good *human* life of the multitude, of a multitude of persons; it is their communion in good living. It is therefore common to both *the whole and the parts* into which it flows back and which, in turn, must benefit from it."[21] For this reason, the common good cannot be reduced to merely the sum of individual goods, and a system that encourages individuals to pursue only their own good will not serve the common good. At the same time, the common good is not merely the good of the collective at the expense of the individual, because the goal of the society is ultimately the material and spiritual flourishing of every person. This flourishing allows the person to reach his ultimate end. A purely materialist understanding of the person, according to the Church, "would end up transforming the common good into simple *socio-economic well-being*, without any transcendental goal, that is, without its most intimate reason for existing".[22] Because it has this transcendent goal, the common good "can be understood as the social and community dimension of the moral good".[23]

[19] Vatican Council II, Pastoral Constitution on the Church in the Modern World, *Gaudium et Spes* (December 7, 1965), no. 26; Paul VI, *Acta Apostolicae Sedis* 58 (1966), no. 1046.

[20] Pontifical Council for Justice and Peace, *Compendium of Social Doctrine* (June 29, 2004), no. 168.

[21] Jacques Maritain, *The Person and the Common Good*, trans. John Fitzgerald (Notre Dame, Ind.: University of Notre Dame Press, 2002), 51. Emphasis in original.

[22] Pontifical Council for Justice and Peace, *Compendium of Social Doctrine*, no. 170. Emphasis in original.

[23] Ibid., no. 164.

The common good is the ultimate end aimed for by the state and the community, but since it concerns the things of this world, it is only a relative end for the person.[24] The person's ultimate end is union with God. Thus, serving the common good cannot put one's ultimate good in jeopardy, and for this reason the common good cannot be separated from the moral good. So, for example, if the state required someone to act in a way harmful to his salvation, that act could not truly be in accord with the common good.

Subsidiarity

An important aspect of both Maurin's and Day's understanding of personalism was an emphasis on personal responsibility, not only a man's responsibility for himself, but also his responsibility for others. As in their understanding of the common good, Maurin and Day embraced the Church's prioritization of the personal above the state in the principle of subsidiarity. This principle is clearly stated by Pope Pius XI:

> Just as it is gravely wrong to take from individuals what they can accomplish by their own initiative and industry and give it to the community, so also it is an injustice and at the same time a grave evil and disturbance of right order to assign to a greater and higher association what lesser and subordinate organizations can do. For every social activity ought of its very nature to furnish help to the members of the body social and never destroy and absorb them.[25]

This principle is further developed in the *Catechism of the Catholic Church*:

---

[24] See Maritain, *Person and Common Good*, 61–64.
[25] Pius XI, *Quadragesimo Anno*, no. 79.

Excessive intervention by the state can threaten personal freedom and initiative. The teaching of the Church has elaborated the principle of *subsidiarity*, according to which "a community of a higher order should not interfere in the internal life of a community of a lower order, depriving the latter of its functions, but rather should support it in case of need and help to co-ordinate its activity with the activities of the rest of society, always with a view to the common good."[26]

Pope Pius XI was concerned that "following upon the overthrow and near extinction of that rich social life which was once highly developed through associations of various kinds, there remain virtually only individuals and the state."[27] This breakdown in community has resulted in the loss of personal responsibility and an increased reliance on the state. This includes the loss of the sense of our personal responsibility for others, and the assumption that they are the state's responsibility. As Pope Francis observed: "Almost without being aware of it, we end up being incapable of feeling compassion at the outcry of the poor, weeping for other people's pain, and feeling a need to help them, as though all this were someone else's responsibility and not out own."[28] Day, in her book *House of Hospitality*, quoted Peter Maurin saying: "Socialism is the state doing things for people instead of people doing things for each other."[29] In *Loaves and Fishes*, Day observed:

[26] *Catechism of the Catholic Church*, 2nd ed. (Vatican City: Libreria Editrice Vaticana; Washington, D.C.: United States Catholic Conference, 2000), no. 1883, citing John Paul II, *Centesimus Annus: On the Hundredth Anniversary of "Rerum Novarum"* (1991), no. 48. The *Catechism* will hereafter be cited as *CCC*.

[27] Pius XI, *Quadragesimo Anno*, no. 78.

[28] Francis, *Evangelii Gaudium* (2013), no. 54.

[29] Dorothy Day, *House of Hospitality* (New York: Sheed and Ward, 1939), 72.

In our country, we have revolted against the poverty and
hunger of the world. Our response has been characteristi-
cally American: we have tried to clean up everything, build
bigger and better shelters and hospitals. Here, hopefully,
misery was to be cared for in an efficient and orderly way.
Yes, we have tried to do much with Holy Mother the State
taking over more and more responsibility for the poor. But
charity is only as warm as those who administer it.[30]

While the principle of subsidiarity raises concerns about
the state taking on too much responsibility, it is also a failure of subsidiarity for citizens to criticize the state without
taking up their own responsibility to help those in need
and to promote the common good.

Distributism

Maurin and Day were convinced that the economic system
that best serves the common good and reflects the principle of subsidiarity is distributism. Prior to their meeting
in 1932, both Day and Maurin had read the writings of
the Russian distributist prince Peter Kropotkin. They were
also influenced by the British writers G.K. Chesterton and
Hilaire Belloc, who both advocated this economic system.
According to Day, "distributism is a system conformable to
the needs of man and his nature."[31] The distributists were
critical of both capitalism and communism (the latter of
which they often referred to as "collectivism") because both
of these systems fail to recognize the proper relationship
between the person and the property by which he earns

[30] Dorothy Day, *Loaves and Fishes* (Maryknoll, N.Y.: Orbis Books, 2007), 74.
[31] Dorothy Day, "Distributism Is Not Dead", *Catholic Worker*, July–August
1956, Catholic Worker Movement website, http://www.catholicworker.org
/dorothyday/articles/244.html.

his living. As we have seen, communism emphasizes state ownership of this property in opposition to private ownership. Capitalism embraces the right to private property but can result in the accumulation of property in the hands of a few. Since the goal of capitalism is the increase of profits, it tends toward monopolies because one increases profits by driving competition out of the market and thus increasing one's own share of the market. As Chesterton observed:

> The practical tendency of all trade and business to-day is towards big commercial combinations, often more imperial, more impersonal, more international than many a communist commonwealth—things that are at least collective if not collectivist. It is all very well to repeat distractedly, "What are we coming to, with all this Bolshevism?" It is equally relevant to add, "What are we coming to, even without Bolshevism?" The obvious answer is—Monopoly. It is certainly not private enterprise.... Monopoly is neither private nor enterprising. It exists to prevent private property.[32]

In other words, as capitalism moves toward multinational corporations, it moves further away from widespread private ownership. Distributists, in contrast, favor private ownership for as many people as possible, not just for the few. Chesterton wrote: "What I complain of, in the current defence of existing capitalism, is that it is a defence of keeping most men in wage dependence: that is, in keeping most men without capital."[33] Distributism maintains that most people should be working for themselves and not for a wage, because in this way one preserves the true dignity of work. Obviously, this call for increased individual ownership is also a rejection of communism's emphasis on state ownership.

[32] G. K. Chesterton, *The Outline of Sanity* (London: Meuthen, 1928), 4.
[33] Ibid., 6–7.

Advocates of distributism were criticized from both sides for being utopian idealists. But Chesterton and Belloc argued that it is not unrealistic idealism, because the system not only existed but flourished in the Middle Ages. Further, Chesterton pointed to examples of the distributist model still working well in the early twentieth century. In his book *Irish Impressions*, first published in 1919, he recounted driving along a country road and seeing that "all down one side of the road, as far as we went, the harvest was gathered in neatly and safely; and all down the other side of the road it was rotting in the rain."[34] When he asked why this was the case, he learned that the fields on one side were all owned by individual families, while those on the other side were part of a large modern estate. The modern estate had had a labor dispute, and the crops were not harvested. The estate owner had more property than he could manage on his own and relied on the wage earners; the wage earners, who did not own the property, had determined it was to their advantage to allow the crop to fail. In Marx' terms, the conflict was a classic example of the bourgeois owner versus the proletarian workers. But Chesterton observed: "The peasant across the road is neither a bourgeois nor a proletarian."[35] The peasant avoided the class struggle by being independent of either class. Chesterton called for just such a third class, a large class of small owners.[36] For the distributist, human production must be brought back to a human scale, which is found in neither the multinational corporation nor state-owned industries. Chesterton drew a conclusion from this example:

[34] G. K. Chesterton, *Irish Impressions* (Norfolk, Va.: IHS, 2002), 34.
[35] Ibid., 35.
[36] Chesterton, *Outline of Sanity*, 86.

For it must be sharply realized that the peasant proprietors succeeded here, not only because they were really proprietors, but because they were only peasants. It was *because* they were on a small scale that they were a great success.... On the left side of the road the big machine had stopped working, *because* it was a big machine. The small men were still working, because they were not machines.[37]

In their writings, both Chesterton and Belloc recognized the difficulty of establishing a distributist system in the face of capitalism and communism. On a practical level, Chesterton encouraged people to support small business that embodied true private ownership, and he noted that this could be done as easily as walking in or out of a shop.[38] He and Belloc agreed that distributism could be achieved again on a large scale only through the moral reawakening of a society committed to the common good. The question then for Peter Maurin and Dorothy Day was how to bring about such a moral reawakening in modern America. Was it possible to promote and to live according to the ideas of Catholic social teaching and philosophy in a way that would serve others and promote the common good? Their answer to that question was the founding of the Catholic Worker movement.

The Catholic Worker Movement

It should be noted that in establishing the Catholic Worker, the goal for Peter Maurin and Dorothy Day was to establish not a political movement but rather a spiritual movement that would address the problems facing their society.

[37] Chesterton, *Irish Impressions*, 36. Emphasis in original.
[38] Chesterton, *Outline of Sanity*, 95.

Peter Maurin envisioned a program that would put the Church's teachings into action. This program included four main points:

1. To reach the man in the street with social teachings of the Church.
2. To build up a lay apostolate through roundtable discussions for the clarification of thought.
3. To found houses of hospitality for the practice of the corporal and spiritual works of mercy.
4. To found farming communes to alleviate unemployment and to serve as agronomic universities.

Dorothy Day participated in all aspects of this program. She was particularly active in the houses of hospitality, where volunteers would live in community with the homeless, providing them with food and a place to stay, and operating soup kitchens to feed the hungry poor in their neighborhoods.

But her primary focus for many years was editing and writing for the newspaper Maurin established in order to achieve the first of these points, to provide a popular format for promulgating the teachings of the Church with regard to social issues.

The *Catholic Worker*

Day was attracted to Maurin's idea of starting a newspaper to present the Church's teachings and the principles of personalism and distributism to everyday workers. Day also saw the paper as an opportunity to continue her work as a journalist focused on social reform. Maurin wanted to call the paper the *Catholic Radical*, but Day insisted on calling the paper the *Catholic Worker* so that its audience of Catholic lay working people would be readily identifiable.

Day approached Paulist Press about printing the newspaper and learned that she could get 2,500 copies of an eight-page tabloid printed for fifty-seven dollars. She earned some of the money with her writing, and friends contributed the rest. On May 1, 1933, the first copy of the *Catholic Worker* appeared. Day and some others went to the large May Day labor rally at Union Square in New York and sold the paper for a penny a copy. They did not sell many papers, but they enjoyed the discussions they had with workers.

The first issue of the paper was made up mostly of Day's articles on the situation of the workers in New York and around the country. She began with a statement outlining the goal of the paper:

> For those who are sitting on park benches in the warm spring sunlight.
>
> For those who are huddling in shelters trying to escape the rain.
>
> For those who are walking the streets in the all but futile search for work.
>
> For those who think that there is no hope for the future, no recognition of their plight—this little paper is addressed.
>
> It is printed to call their attention to the fact that the Catholic Church has a social program—to let them know that there are men of God who are working not only for their spiritual, but for their material welfare....
>
> In an attempt to popularize and make known the encyclicals of the Popes in regard to social justice and the program put forth by the Church for the "reconstruction of the social order," this new sheet, *The Catholic Worker*, is started.[39]

[39] Dorothy Day, "To Our Readers", *Catholic Worker*, May 1933, Catholic Worker Movement website, http://www.catholicworker.org/dorothyday/articles/12.html.

The first edition of the paper also included essays by Peter Maurin, of the sort that came to be known as his "Easy Essays". In these essays Maurin tried to take his ideas and the ideas of the thinkers he had read and put them simply, quickly, and clearly in a language that anyone could understand. Here is an example:

Personalist Communitarianism

> A personalist
> is a go-giver
> not a go-getter.
>
> He tries to give
> what he has
> and does not
> try to get
> what the other fellow has.
>
> He tries to be good
> by doing good
> to the other fellow.
>
> He is other-centered
> not self-centered.
> He has a social doctrine
> of the common good.
>
> He spreads the social doctrine
> of the common good
> through words and deeds.
>
> He speaks through deeds
> as well as words.

> Through words and deeds
> he brings into existence
> a common unity
> the common unity
> of a community.[40]

Peter Maurin was not completely happy with the first issue of the *Catholic Worker* and asked that his name be withdrawn from the editorial board, though he would still publish in the paper as a contributor. Later Day recalled:

> Much later, when I had looked at the first issue, I could see more clearly what bothered Peter. We had emphasized wages and hours while he was trying to talk about a philosophy of work. I had written of women in industry, children in industry, of sweatshops and strikes.... It must have appeared to him that we were just urging the patching-up of the industrial system instead of trying to rebuild society itself with a philosophy so old it seemed like new.[41]

They may not have sold many copies of that first edition, but the paper rapidly grew in popularity. Within four months the circulation was 25,000; by 1936 it had increased to 150,000.[42]

[40] Peter Maurin, "Personalist Communitarianism", quoted in Dorothy Day, *Peter Maurin: Apostle to the World*, with Francis J. Sicius (Maryknoll, N.Y.: Orbis Books, 2004), 77–78. An audio recording of Peter Maurin reading one of his Easy Essays ("Makers of Europe", or "When the Irish Were Irish" [ca. 1939]) is available at the Internet Archive, "Peter Maurin Speaks", http://www.archive.org/details/petermaurin.

[41] Day, *Loaves and Fishes*, 22.

[42] Dorothy Day, *The Long Loneliness* (New York: Harper and Brothers, 1952), 182.

The *Catholic Worker* is still being published today and still sells for one cent a copy. The name of the paper has also become attached to the larger Catholic Worker movement, which has spread around the world.

Chapter Four

DAY'S SPIRITUALITY, PART I: SCRIPTURE AND SAINTS

In the last chapter we considered several of the ideas that shaped Dorothy Day's understanding of the program necessary to achieve the goals of the Catholic Worker movement. In this chapter we will consider the foundations and development of Day's spirituality.[1] Some who knew Day have observed that many of those who praise her social activism and her work for peace and justice are reluctant to acknowledge the spiritual foundation of her work. As Sister Peter Claver Fahy, whom Day credits with donating the first dollar to the Catholic Worker, observed, "They won't give God the credit."[2] But any attempt to understand Day and the Catholic Worker movement must consider the spiritual forces that made her work possible. In this chapter we will consider two influences on her spirituality: Scripture and the saints. In this we are following the guidance of Day herself, who wrote: "The best thing to do in the cause of our redemption and real freedom is to

[1] For an in-depth account of Day's spirituality, see Brigid O'Shea Merriman, *Searching for Christ: The Spirituality of Dorothy Day* (Notre Dame, Ind.: University of Notre Dame Press, 1994).
[2] Quoted in Mark and Louise Zwick, *The Catholic Worker Movement: Intellectual and Spiritual Origins* (New York: Paulist, 2005), 248.

read the Scriptures. Then read what the canonized saints have to say."[3]

Scripture

After her conversion, Day made reading Scripture a part of her daily routine. Even prior to her conversion, she was drawn to the psalms for comfort while she was in jail. Throughout her life Day continued to read and meditate on the psalms, which she felt often reflected the cries to God from those in need of help. She found C. S. Lewis' *Reflections on the Psalms* particularly helpful in understanding them. She discovered that reading the psalms as part of the daily Divine Office provided her with a storehouse of wisdom she could draw upon when faced with difficulties.

Day's spirituality was also grounded in the New Testament, particularly the Gospel of Saint Matthew. Maybe the most important passage for Day, the one she referred to most often in her life and her writing, is the account of the last judgment found in Matthew 25:31–46, where Jesus says:

> When the Son of man comes in his glory, and all the angels with him, then he will sit on his glorious throne. Before him will be gathered all the nations, and he will separate them one from another as a shepherd separates the sheep from the goats, and he will place the sheep at his right hand, but the goats at the left. Then the King will say to those at his right hand, "Come, O blessed of my Father, inherit the kingdom prepared for you from the foundation of the world; for I was hungry and you

[3] Quoted in William D. Miller, *All Is Grace: The Spirituality of Dorothy Day* (Garden City, N.Y.: Doubleday, 1987), 117.

gave me food, I was thirsty and you gave me drink, I was a stranger and you welcomed me, I was naked and you clothed me, I was sick and you visited me, I was in prison and you came to me." Then the righteous will answer him, "Lord, when did we see you hungry and feed you, or thirsty and give you drink? And when did we see you a stranger and welcome you, or naked and clothe you? And when did we see you sick or in prison and visit you?" And the King will answer them, "Truly, I say to you, as you did it to one of the least of these my brethren, you did it to me." Then he will say to those at his left hand, "Depart from me, you cursed, into the eternal fire prepared for the devil and his angels; for I was hungry and you gave me no food, I was thirsty and you gave me no drink, I was a stranger and you did not welcome me, naked and you did not clothe me, sick and in prison and you did not visit me." Then they will answer, "Lord, when did we see you hungry or thirsty or a stranger or naked or sick or in prison, and did not minister to you?" Then he will answer them, "Truly, I say to you, as you did it not to one of the least of these, you did it not to me." And they will go away into the eternal punishment, but the righteous into eternal life.

From this passage Day understood that Jesus will separate those who will be punished from those who will join Him in eternal life based on their treatment of "the least" among us—that is to say, the hungry, the naked, the sick, the stranger, and the prisoner.

She completely embraced the idea that what one does for those who suffer in these ways one does for Christ Himself, and that when one ignores those who are suffering, one is in fact ignoring Christ. Day's ability to see Jesus Christ in all those she met, and particularly in those who were the outcasts of society, was the center of her spirituality. The works of mercy that are rooted in this

Gospel passage became the foundation and the heart of the Catholic Worker movement.

The Sermon on the Mount was also foundational for Day. Her pacifism was based on the Beatitudes (Mt 5:3–12), where Jesus identifies those who show mercy and pursue peace as among the blessed. Her commitment to the poor and her pacifism were also rooted in the letters of Saint Paul and their teachings about the mystical body of Christ. Her embrace of the idea that all are one in the body of Christ led her to relieve suffering and to condemn violence wherever she encountered them.

One of Day's favorite Scripture passages was the story of the loaves and the fishes. It was one that she often referred to, and in fact she published a book about her life in the Catholic Worker movement entitled *Loaves and Fishes*. She was particularly drawn to the version of the miracle as it is presented in the Gospel of John, where the source of the fish and bread is a young boy who gives everything he has to Christ. She compared her work and the work of the Catholic Worker to the boy who really did not have much to give but whose meager gifts were used by Christ to perform great things.

The Saints

Even prior to her conversion, Day was drawn not only to Scripture but to the lives and the writings of the saints. As we have seen, she chose her daughter's middle name, Teresa, in honor of Saint Teresa of Avila. Earlier she had also been interested in the writings of Saint Francis of Assisi. After her conversion, Day explored the lives of the saints in greater detail, and several holy men and women became important influences in her life. Here we will look at three saints whose influence was particularly keen: Saint Benedict, Saint Francis, and Saint Thérèse of Lisieux.

Saint Benedict of Nursia (ca. 480–ca. 550)

Saint Benedict is best known as the father of Western monasticism. The rule he wrote around 530 for the monks at his monastery at Monte Cassino is the foundation for most Christian monastic orders. Day was greatly influenced by the rule's understanding of hospitality and its theology of work.

At the time of Saint Benedict it was not unusual for travelers and pilgrims to seek hospitality at a monastery. Saint Benedict is very clear about the hospitality that the monastery should extend to all who arrive at its doors as guests. In chapter 53 of his rule he says: "All guests who present themselves are to be welcomed as Christ, for he himself will say: *I was a stranger and you welcomed me.*"[4] Further, all guests are to be met with "the courtesy of love". Benedict emphasizes that guests must be treated with respect because Christ is present in them, and he thinks this is particularly true of the poor. He says: "Great care and concern are to be shown in receiving poor people and pilgrims, because in them more particularly is Christ received."[5] Day and Peter Maurin operated their houses for the poor with this spirit of hospitality.

The people who sought their help were always welcomed and referred to as guests, and the explicit foundation of this hospitality is the identification of Christ with those seeking shelter and assistance. Day observes that hospitality should be given "not because these people remind

---

[4] Benedict, *The Rule of Saint Benedict in English*, ed. Timothy Fry (New York: Vintage Books, 1998), 51. Emphasis in original.

[5] Ibid., 51–52.

us of Christ ... but because they *are* Christ".[6] Similarly,
Saint Benedict prescribes the way that a monk should welcome the guest: "By a bow of the head or by a complete
prostration of the body, Christ is to be adored because he
is indeed welcomed in them."[7] For this reason, Day always
claimed that one does not serve the poor out of duty but
out of love of Christ, whom they embody. She says: "It
is not a duty to help Christ, it is a privilege."[8] Near the
end of her life, Day drew the following conclusion about
hospitality: "All Christians are called to be hospitable. But
it is more than serving a meal or filling a bed, opening
the door—it is to open ourselves, our hearts to the needs
of others. Hospitality is not just shelter, but the quality of
welcome behind it."[9]

Day and Maurin were also drawn to the relationship
between work and spirituality found in Saint Benedict.
The famous motto of the Benedictines, "Pray and work"
(*Ora et labora*), is not meant to divide these activities but
to emphasize their connection. In chapter 48 of the rule,
Saint Benedict observes: "Idleness is the enemy of the soul.
Therefore, the brothers have specific periods for manual
labor as well as for prayerful reading."[10] This chapter goes
on to prescribe in detail the order and the integration of
manual labor, spiritual reading, and praying the Divine
Office. The labor discussed in the rule of Saint Benedict
included activities such as sowing and harvesting, and also
works of mercy such as tending to sick brothers. Manual

[6] Dorothy Day, "Room for Christ", in *Dorothy Day: Selected Writings*, ed.
Robert Ellsberg (Maryknoll, N.Y.: Orbis Books, 1993), 97.

[7] Benedict, *Rule*, 51.

[8] Day, "Room for Christ", in *Day: Selected Writings*, 97.

[9] Dorothy Day, "Going to the Roots ... Questions and Answers", *Catholic
Worker*, May 1978, quoted in Merriman, *Searching for Christ*, 92.

[10] Benedict, *Rule*, 47.

work was seen by the monks as a way of both glorifying God and supporting themselves so that they could do the work of God—prayer and the sacraments.

Prayer, daily Mass, and the Eucharist were essential to Day's approach to the Catholic Worker. As Brigid Merriman observed, Day "believed firmly that prayer was the first duty of all those working for social justice, and only that which was done for Christ and with Christ was of value".[11] For Day, the work was important, but it had to flow from prayer and not be given priority over prayer. Merriman reports that Day, "in addressing a group of would-be Catholic Workers in the early 1940s, admonished them 'the Mass is the work!' All their activities were first to be offered and united frequently with the sacrifice of Christ on the cross and on the altar."[12] In an article from 1962, Day writes:

> Our need to worship, to praise, to give thanksgiving, makes us return to the Mass daily, as the only fitting worship which we can offer to God. Having received our God in the consecrated bread and wine, which still to sense is bread and wine, it is now not we ourselves who do these things except by virtue of the fact that we will to do them, and put ourselves in the position to do them by coming to the Holy Sacrifice, receiving communion, and then with Christ in our hearts and literally within us in the bread we have received, giving this praise, honor and glory and thanksgiving....
>
> But the Mass begins our day, it is our food and drink, our delight, our refreshment, our courage, our light.[13]

[11] Merriman, *Searching for Christ*, 97.
[12] Ibid.
[13] Dorothy Day, "The Council and the Mass", *Catholic Worker*, September 1962, Catholic Worker Movement website, http://www.catholicworker.org /dorothyday/articles/794.html.

A few years later she observed: "I would not dare write or speak or try to follow the vocation God has given me to work for the poor and for peace if I did not have this constant reassurance of the Mass."[14]

Throughout her life Day drew insight and encouragement for her work through the teachings of Saint Benedict. Day's affinity for the Benedictine integration of work and prayer was confirmed when she was professed a Benedictine Oblate on April 26, 1955.

Saint Francis of Assisi (1182–1226)

A second saint who had a profound influence on Day was Saint Francis of Assisi. In particular he shaped her understanding of poverty and nonviolence. Day began reading about the life of Saint Francis shortly after her conversion, and her interest was deepened by Peter Maurin's attraction to the saint. Both were strongly influenced by Pope Pius XI's encyclical on Saint Francis, *Rite Expiatis*, which he issued in 1926. In this encyclical the Holy Father affirms Saint Francis as a model of Catholic action in a turbulent time. He also cautions us not to reduce the saint to merely popular pious sentiments: "As the Herald of the Great King, his [Saint Francis'] purposes were directed to persuading men to conform their lives to the dictates of evangelical sanctity and to the love of the Cross, not that they should become mere friends or lovers of flowers, birds, lambs, fishes or hares."[15] Indeed, Day and Maurin were interested not in the "birdbath" image of the saint but rather in his radical embrace of the Gospel message.

[14] Dorothy Day, "On Pilgrimage", *Catholic Worker*, March 1966, Catholic Worker Movement website, http://catholicworker.org/dorothyday/articles/249.html.

[15] Pius XI, *Rite Expiatis* (1926), no. 40.

One of the central aspects of Saint Francis' life and thought was his embrace of poverty. Pius XI quotes Saint Bonaventure, who said of Saint Francis: "No one was ever so eager for gold as he was for poverty."[16] The Pope describes this as "evangelical poverty", which renounces the acquisition of the material things of this world in order to bring oneself more clearly in accord with the message of the Gospels and in this way bring that message into the world. Saint Francis, the son of a wealthy merchant, felt that God had drawn him to the passages in the Gospels about the wealthy young man who is instructed by Christ to sell all he has in order to follow Him (Mt 19:16–30). But unlike the young man in Scripture, Saint Francis embraces this counsel.

Often in the *Catholic Worker* and other writings, Day advocated the embrace of voluntary poverty, which she understood as central to the entire Catholic Worker movement. Day recognizes the seeming paradox of working to alleviate poverty while at the same time calling for the embrace of poverty. But she says the confusion arises from not understanding "the difference between inflicted poverty and voluntary poverty; between being victims and champions of poverty. I prefer to call the one kind *destitution*, reserving the word *poverty* for what St. Francis called 'Lady Poverty'."[17] For Day, voluntary poverty was important because when we become too insulated in our comforts, the reality of others' poverty fades, and we lose sight of it and of our obligation to the poor. But poverty is important for one's own relationship to the world and ability to bear witness to the Gospel in the world.

---

[16] Ibid., no. 15.
[17] Dorothy Day, *Loaves and Fishes* (Maryknoll, N.Y.: Orbis Books, 1997), 82.

The act and spirit of giving are the best counter to the evil forces in the world today, and giving liberates the individual not only spiritually but materially. For, in a world [of] enslavement through installment buying and mortgages, the only way to live in any true security is to live so close to the bottom that when you fall you do not have far to drop, you do not have much to lose.

And in a world of hates and fears, we can look to Peter Maurin's words for the liberation that love brings: "Voluntary poverty is the answer. We cannot see our brother in need without stripping ourselves. It is the only way we have of showing our love."[18]

Those in the Catholic Worker movement who volunteer in the houses of hospitality live in community with the "guests" they shelter and do not receive a salary but practice voluntary poverty and live on the donations they receive from those who choose to support their work. Day and the others frequently experienced the precariousness of the poor, who often have bills to pay and no money in the bank. But Day never lost sight of the fact that she and the volunteers chose to live this way. Day also recognized the difficulty of embracing a life of voluntary poverty and that many who attempted it often quickly abandoned it. For this reason she advised that people might be better off gradually reducing their acquisition of and attachment to material things.[19]

Day was also influenced by Saint Francis' teachings on nonviolence. Saint Francis had been a soldier prior to his conversion, and he had experienced the violence

[18] Ibid., 86.
[19] Dorothy Day, "Poverty without Tears", *Catholic Worker*, April 1950, Catholic Worker Movement website, http://www.catholicworker.org/dorothyday/articles/230.html.

that was often employed in his world. After his conversion he embraced the Gospel message of peace, which he impressed upon his followers, men and women, who joined the orders he founded. As Pope Pius XI observed: "The principal desire which filled these new preachers of penance was to help bring back peace not only to individuals but to families, cities, and even nations, torn by interminable wars and steeped in blood."[20] This was particularly important for third-order Franciscans, as the lay followers of Saint Francis are called. At the time of Francis, the laity joined the third order in such large numbers that it diminished the nobles' ability to wage war since members of the order were not permitted to bear arms, except in the defense of the Roman Church and the Christian faith, and they could not be conscripted for military service. Without armies at their disposal, kings and princes had to negotiate their differences. In this way, Saint Francis transformed the feudal system and reduced the number of armed conflicts. Day saw in Saint Francis a model of how the Gospel message of peace could be brought to a violent world, and his peacemaking efforts helped to shape her teachings on pacifism, which will be discussed in detail in chapter 7.

Saint Thérèse of Lisieux (1873–1897)

Day's initial encounter with Saint Thérèse of Lisieux was in the hospital following the birth of her daughter. This was prior to Day's conversion to Catholicism, and she was still largely ignorant of the Church's saints and practices. One of the young mothers in the maternity ward was Catholic, and when she heard that Day's daughter's middle name

[20] Pius XI, *Rite Expiatis*, no. 33.

was Teresa, she gave Day a medal of the Little Flower for the baby. She accepted the gift but recalled: "I was some years from being a Catholic and I shied away from this evidence of superstition and charm-wearing. I wanted no such talisman."[21]

Day's second encounter with the Little Flower was in 1928. Father Zachary, her confessor, gave her a copy of Saint Thérèse's autobiography, *The Story of a Soul*. But Day admits that her first impression of the young saint was not favorable.

> She was very young and her writing seemed to me like that of a school girl. I wasn't looking for anything so simple and felt slightly aggrieved at Fr. Zachary. Men, and priests too, were very insulting to women, I thought, handing out what they felt suited their intelligence; in other words, pious pap. I dutifully read *The Story of a Soul* and am ashamed to confess that I found it colorless, monotonous, too small in fact for my notice.[22]

At the time Day acknowledged that her image of a saint was much more that of Joan of Arc leading an army than of a young cloistered nun doing the laundry. Over the next thirty years, however, her views changed to the extent that she researched and wrote a book on Saint Thérèse, which she published in 1960. What was it about her experience in the Catholic Worker movement that led her to reevaluate her first impression of the Little Flower and to embrace her as one of her most important spiritual teachers?

Through her work with the poor, Day came to understand that it is the small things that we do every day that

---

[21] Dorothy Day, *Thérèse: A Life of Thérèse of Lisieux* (Notre Dame, Ind.: Fides Publishers Association, 1960), vi.

[22] Ibid., viii.

reveal our love of God and the ways in which God is at work in and through us. She realized that her work resembled Saint Thérèse's "Little Way". Day wrote: "What did she do? She practiced the presence of God and she did all things—all the little things that make up our daily life and contact with others—for His honor and glory."[23] The Little Way is not a method but an attitude placing complete trust in God and seeking to reflect the love of God in every action it does. With this in mind, Day realized that all of our struggles, even our apparent failures, take on a new light. Merriman maintained that from Saint Thérèse, Day "learned greater confidence in the ultimate effectiveness of small actions, when strengthened by prayer and the support of others".[24] This confidence empowered Day to go on with her work even though the number of hungry people seemed always to increase and the Catholic Worker was criticized for being only a "band-aid" that did nothing to solve the problems of the poor. In an interview in 1973, Day offered this reflection: "For me the heart of our work is just that, the daily pastoral responsibilities: making the soup and serving it, trying to help someone get to the hospital who otherwise might not get there, because he's confused, because she's not aware she even needs to go there."[25] For Day, her commitment was not to fight for justice or human rights in the abstract but to act in the concrete local scene where she found herself. Day realized that in the face of criticism or despair at the enormity of a task, she needed the hope and joy that came through the Little Way, and

[23] Ibid., 174.

[24] Merriman, *Searching for Christ*, 197.

[25] Robert Coles, *Dorothy Day: A Radical Devotion* (Boston: Da Capo, 1987), 102.

this realization is what led her to write her book about Saint Thérèse. As she explained in the preface:

> I wrote to overcome the sense of futility in Catholics, men, women, and youths, married and single, who feel hopeless and useless, less than the dust, ineffectual, wasted, powerless. On the one hand Therese was "the little grain of sand" and on the other "her name was written in heaven"; she was beloved by her heavenly Father, she was the bride of Christ, she was little less than the angels. And so are we all.[26]

Day came to understand that it was important not to see great or immediate results from our actions but to know that when we trust in God, he will always be at work in everything we do, and thus nothing we do is ever in vain. Day was impatient with those volunteers who wanted to change the world but did not want to chop the vegetables. She knew that being young and idealistic is a good thing, but as she grew older she came to understand that somebody has to chop the vegetables every day or the soup does not get made and people go hungry. Day once referred to Saint Thérèse as "the Saint of the responsible".[27] Day recognized that it was the saint's very "smallness", her very ordinariness, that made her so beloved by people from all walks of life.

[26] Day, *Thérèse*, xii.
[27] Dorothy Day, "No Party Line", *Catholic Worker*, April 1952, Catholic Worker Movement website, http://www.catholicworker.org/dorothyday /articles/184.html.

Chapter Five

DAY'S SPIRITUALITY, PART II: THE CHURCH

Day's experience of the Catholic Church was a vital part of her spiritual formation. In the first part we will consider Day's understanding of obedience and authority and her relationship to Church hierarchy. We will consider her appreciation of the Church's moral teachings and how two contemporary movements in the Church, the Liturgical Movement and the Lacouture retreat experience, contributed to her spiritual growth.

Authority, Obedience, and Conscience

Day's relationship to the Catholic Church of her day was not always an easy one; it was complex and at times paradoxical. But it would be incorrect to draw from the points of conflict that Day was a dissenting Catholic. Day loved the Church and was obedient to it. She never ceased to see the Church as her Holy Mother. In an article from 1966 reflecting on the nature of obedience, she wrote: "Obedience is a matter of love, which makes it voluntary, not compelled by fear or force."[1] She speculated that as a

[1] Dorothy Day, "Reflections during Advent", pt. 4, "Obedience", *Ave Maria*, December 17, 1966, Catholic Worker Movement website, http://www.catholicworker.org/dorothyday/articles/562.html.

convert she had a greater understanding of her obedience to the Church because she clearly chose it. "Most cradle Catholics have gone through, or need to go through, a second conversion which binds them with a more profound, a more mature love and obedience to the Church."[2] She also noted that her own seeking for faith when she was young made her appreciate the gift of faith and the gift of the Church. This gratitude created in her a desire to follow the Church's teachings. Thus, for Day, obedience to the Church was a natural outgrowth of her faith.

In an article from 1970 Day took up the question of the relationship between conscience and obedience and expressed her agreement with the Church's understanding of conscience as articulated by the Second Vatican Council.[3] This understanding is expressed in *Gaudium et Spes*: "In the depths of his conscience, man detects a law which he has not laid upon himself, but which holds him in obedience.... For man has in his heart a law written by God."[4] According to the *Catechism of the Catholic Church*, conscience rightly understood is a judgment of reason by which a person "perceives and recognizes the prescriptions of the divine law".[5] This rational understanding of the divine law is what the Church calls natural law. Thus, the goal of conscience is to discern the truth so as "to be guided by the objective standards of moral conduct".[6] That is to say, the conscience is not itself the authority,

[2] Ibid.

[3] See Dorothy Day, "On Pilgrimage—Our Spring Appeal", *Catholic Worker*, May 1970, Catholic Worker Movement website, http://www.catholicworker .org/dorothyday/articles/500.html.

[4] Vatican Council II, Pastoral Constitution on the Church in the Modern World, *Gaudium et Spes* (December 7, 1965), no. 16.

[5] *CCC* 1778. See also Vatican Council II, Declaration on Religious Liberty, *Dignitatis Humanae* (December 7, 1965), no. 3.

[6] *Gaudium et Spes*, no. 16.

but rather the truth is the authority the conscience seeks to understand. Conscience should not be misunderstood as a feeling that one has about a moral issue or as a justification for the claim that the moral law is relative to each individual. As Pope John Paul II observed: "The conscience, therefore, is not an independent and exclusive capacity to decide what is good and what is evil."[7] Conscience properly understood is the use of our rational faculties directed toward the understanding of the objective moral truth. The Church also emphasizes the importance of a well-formed conscience: "A well formed conscience is upright and truthful. It formulates its judgments according to reason, in conformity with the true good willed by the wisdom of the Creator."[8] Further: "In the formation of conscience the Word of God is the light for our path, we must assimilate it in faith and prayer and put it into practice. We must examine our conscience before the Lord's Cross. We are assisted by the gifts of the Holy Spirit, aided by the witness or advice of others and guided by the authoritative teaching of the Church."[9]

Individuals are responsible for the proper formation of their conscience. Acts that violate the objective moral law, if done as a result of an ignorant or an ill-formed conscience, are regarded as sinful if the individual is responsible for this ignorance or inadequate formation. Further, as Pope John Paul II observed: "It is never acceptable to confuse a 'subjective' error about moral good with the 'objective' truth rationally proposed to man in virtue of his end, or to make the moral value of an act performed

[7]John Paul II, *Dominum et Vivificantem: On the Holy Spirit in the Life of the Church and the World* (1986), no. 43. Cf. John Paul II, *Fides et Ratio: On the Relationship between Faith and Reason* (1998), no. 98.

[8] CCC 1783.

[9] CCC 1785.

with a true and correct conscience equivalent to the moral value of an act performed by following the judgment of an erroneous conscience."[10] Thus, one's conscience should never be understood as an infallible faculty.

Dorothy Day explained her acts of civil disobedience and opposition to some uses of state authority with an appeal to conscience. She believed that she was not bound by obedience to a law if it violated the moral law. For example, as early as 1940 Day opposed the conscription laws with regard to drafting men into the military, and her opposition to these laws continued through the Vietnam War. As a pacifist, Day viewed war as immoral and thus believed that the state could not require men to serve in the military. She therefore encouraged men to resist the draft through an appeal to conscience.

Day was also aware of the relationship between conscience and obedience with regard to the authority of the Church. She recounted how, when she was considering whether she should start the *Catholic Worker* newspaper, she asked three priests whom she knew whether she needed to get permission before starting the venture. All three told her the same thing, that she did not need permission and that if God wanted the paper to succeed, it would. She said this gave her a real sense of freedom to say what she wanted without fear that she would be seen as speaking for the Church hierarchy: if she made a mistake, it would not cause as much harm as if she were speaking officially for the Church and were a cause of scandal. Day writes that she was "grateful for the freedom we had in the Church" and that she "was quite ready to obey with cheerfulness if Cardinal Spellman [the archbishop of New York] ever told us to lay down our pens and stop

---

[10] John Paul II, *Veritatis Splendor* (1993), no. 63.

publication".[11] Day's pledge of obedience surprised many, and some challenged her claim, but she reaffirmed her position and responded to her critics: "My answer would be (and it is an easier one to make now that the Council has spoken so clearly) that my respect for Cardinal Spellman and my faith that God will right all mistakes, mine as well as his, would lead me to obey."[12] Father Richard McSoreley, a friend of Day's, speculated that the cardinal knew that Day would be obedient, so he saw no reason to put it to a test through a confrontation that could only be harmful.[13] Her positions did at times put her at odds with others within the Church, including its leadership. But from Day's perspective these conflicts only reflected the freedom that was possible in the Church, and gave rise to opportunities to come to a clearer understanding. In an interview from 1964 Day observed: "I found such infinite freedom in the Church, really. And all these controversies, it seems to me, as Peter [Maurin] always used to point out, were only for the clarification of thought. It just seems to me to be your conscience at work."[14] She expressed similar views in private, as, for example, in a letter from 1960 in which she writes: "The Church means everything to me. It is Christ Himself. I know I could not be asked to do anything against my conscience."[15] The hierarchy, for

[11] Day, "Reflections during Advent", pt. 4, "Obedience".

[12] Dorothy Day, "On Pilgrimage", *Catholic Worker*, December 1965, Catholic Worker Movement website, http://www.catholicworker.org/dorothyday/articles/248.pdf.

[13] Rosalie Riegle, *Dorothy Day: Portraits by Those Who Knew Her* (Maryknoll, N.Y.: Orbis Books, 2003), 98.

[14] John T. Catoir, *Encounters with Holiness* (New York: Society of St. Paul, 2007), 35.

[15] Dorothy Day to Deane Mary Mowrer, April 7, 1960, in *All the Way to Heaven: The Selected Letters of Dorothy Day*, ed. Robert Ellsberg (Milwaukee, Wis.: Marquette University Press, 2010), 262.

its part, always apprised Day privately of any concerns regarding things she wrote or did.[16]

Day accepted the Church's teachings on faith and morals but thought that in the areas of economics or sociology, debate and disagreement were permitted and should be encouraged to help clarify thinking. One of Day's most public confrontations with the Church hierarchy was over a strike by the gravediggers' union in 1949. Cardinal Spellman ordered seminarians to dig the graves in order to break the strike. Day joined the strikers in picketing the archbishop's office, and in the paper she described his actions as "ill advised".[17] The strike collapsed, and Day was disappointed. Some wanted Day and the *Catholic Worker* reprimanded for this stand, but the cardinal never took any punitive action against her or the newspaper.

When Day was critical of the Church, it was not from the perspective that it should change its teachings but rather from the perspective that it needed to embrace more fully these teachings and the teachings of the Gospels. She was frustrated that the Church and its members did not better employ their resources to help the poor. For example, in a letter from 1935 to Monsignor Arthur Scanlan, the censor for the Archdiocese of New York, she defended an article in the *Catholic Worker* that some had read as critical of the Church:

> In the interest of Catholic motherhood, we wished to point out all that is being done to give free, or reasonably cheap care to mothers in the way of clinics and hospitals,

[16] See Dorothy Day, "The Case of Cardinal McIntyre", *Catholic Worker*, July–August 1964, Catholic Worker Movement website, http://www.catholic worker.org/dorothyday/articles/196.html.

[17] Dorothy Day, "On Pilgrimage", *Catholic Worker*, April 1949, Catholic Worker Movement website, http://www.catholicworker.org/dorothyday/articles/493.html.

prenatal and post-natal care.... We call attention to the
need of it and even the lack of recognition of this problem
and lack of constructive work done along these lines, so
perhaps that is what antagonizes. You cannot campaign
for such things as baby clinics and maternity wards without revealing the fact that there is a dearth of such conve-
niences for Catholic women who are forced to go to city
clinics where they are often handed birth control information and advised, even commanded, to make use of it.[18]

Day followed up this article in 1936 with a piece entitled "The Family vs. Capitalism", where she wrote: "We
cannot understand, then, the shortsightedness of Catholics
who contribute generously for Catholic schools and neglect
to aid the Catholic family life from which the schools must
draw their students.... We have often commented, in *The
Catholic Worker*, on the high cost of maternity care here
and the lack of facilities for such care under Catholic aus-
pices."[19] For Day, the Church was not an abstract entity or
institution but a body of believers who were all responsible
for making the Gospels concrete.

Similarly, Day was scandalized when she saw priests who
seemed to care more about their own worldly comforts
than about the poor and the oppressed, or when Church
leaders seemed too closely bound to capitalism or mili-
tarism. She was impatient with clericalism and was critical of priests who showed scorn for the laity, particularly
women.[20] But she was also impatient with laity who failed
in their obligations to the poor or were overly materialistic.

[18] Dorothy Day to Msgr. Arthur Scanlan, March 16, 1935, in *All the Way to
Heaven*, 72–73.

[19] Dorothy Day, "The Family vs. Capitalism", *Catholic Worker*, January
1936, Catholic Worker Movement website, http://www.catholicworker.org
/dorothyday/articles/142.html.

[20] See Dorothy Day to Fr. Harvey Egan, Easter Week 1954, in *All the Way
to Heaven*, 221–25.

She was fond of quoting from Romano Guardini: the Church is the Cross on which Christ was crucified.[21] That is to say that Christ created the Church, but all of its members, including its priests, leaders, and laity, are imperfect sinners. In an interview with Robert Coles near the end of Day's life, she reflected on this paradox:

> If the church were made up of people who weren't hypocrites and who weren't convinced that they are God's chosen personal emissaries, full of every virtue and free of every vice, then it wouldn't be the church it was meant to be, a church of sinners. You can see that I'm caught in a bind here; I want the church to be less sinful, but I know we are all sinners, and I know I'm taking a chance on becoming one of the worst sinners by denouncing so many of the other sinners around.[22]

In a similar vein she told Coles: "I did not convert with my eyes closed. I knew the Catholic Church had plenty of sin within it. How could there *not* be sin within a church made up of men and women?"[23]

But Day also realized that although at times the Church is a cross, Christ cannot be separated from this cross. Without the Church, without the sacraments, Christ would have been absent from her life. She appreciated the Church's human limitations while calling for its members, including herself, to live more in keeping with Church teachings. And while Day may have been critical of particular clergy, she had a great love and respect for the

---

[21] See, for example, Dorothy Day, *The Long Loneliness* (New York: Harper and Brothers, 1952), 150.

[22] Robert Coles, *Dorothy Day: A Radical Devotion* (Cambridge, Mass.: Da Capo, 1987), 70.

[23] Ibid., 85.

priesthood. She once observed: "We know that through her [the Church's] priests we receive our rebirth in Christ, our communions, our healings of soul and body. She witnesses our marriages and helps us to die and our priests are ordained for these great and noble duties of bringing to us the sacraments, the means of grace which enables us to begin to truly live."[24] Beyond bringing us the sacraments, the priest is also responsible for spiritually feeding the faithful. According to Day: "The first job of the priest ... is not only to give us the sacraments, but also to give us some knowledge of what the sacraments really mean, and how the sacraments feed the soul."[25] Many priests and seminarians found Day to be a great source of inspiration, and they often supported her work in the Catholic Worker movement. By the end of her life, Day was well respected and even revered by members of the Church hierarchy who would seek her input, particularly in matters of social justice.

Day and Church Teachings

While some may have interpreted her words or actions as a challenge to the Church's authority, Day is clear that this was never her purpose:

> I didn't ever see myself as posing a challenge to church authority. I was a Catholic then, and I am one now, and I hope and pray I die one. I have not wanted to challenge the church, not on any of its doctrinal positions. I try to

[24] Dorothy Day, "The Fifth Anniversary of Peter Maurin's Death", *Catholic Worker*, June 1954, Catholic Worker Movement website, http://www.catholicworker.org/dorothyday/articles/669.html.

[25] Catoir, *Encounters with Holiness*, 43.

be loyal to the church—to its teachings, its ideals. I love
the church with all my heart and soul. I never go inside
a church without thanking God Almighty for giving
me a home. The church *is* my home, and I don't want to
be homeless.[26]

As her biographer Jim Forest observed: "Dorothy's
own commitment to the Catholic Church was never at
issue—she wasn't window shopping for another, 'better'
Church. In fact it disturbed many people, including many
in the Catholic Worker movement, that Dorothy was so
conservative a Catholic—so wholehearted in her acceptance of Catholic teaching and structure."[27] Day resented
it when others assumed that because she opposed war
or advanced workers' rights, she must also be critical of
the Church's teachings. In a letter from 1952, she wrote:
"I hate being used as a club to beat the Church and
the hierarchy over the head with. I am a loyal Catholic
and please God intend to remain one to the end of my
days. I have no reservations when I say I mean obedient
Catholic.... I have a hard time getting these ideas into
the heads of liberals like Harpers, Sugrue, Macdonald,
Eichenberg, etc."[28]

In fact, there is much evidence in Day's writings of her
support of the Church's doctrinal teachings, including
those that were not popular with "progressive" critics of

[26] Coles, *Dorothy Day*, 82.

[27] Jim Forest, *All Is Grace: A Biography of Dorothy Day* (Maryknoll, N.Y.:
Orbis Books, 2012), 332.

[28] Dorothy Day to Ammon Hennacy, January 1952, in *All the Way to Heaven*,
202. Harpers is a reference to Day's publisher, Harper & Brothers, which published *The Long Loneliness* in 1952. Thomas Joseph Sugrue (1907–1953) wrote
the book *A Catholic Speaks His Mind on America's Religious Conflict* which Day
reviewed in the *Catholic Worker* in April 1952. Dwight Macdonald (1906–1982)
was a writer who had interviewed Day for the *New Yorker*. Fritz Eichenberg
(1901–1990) was an artist who did many of the illustrations for the *Catholic Worker*.

the Church. For example, she always expressed her support for the Church's teachings on sexuality, chastity, birth control, and abortion. In an article from 1966 reflecting on chastity, she praised sex within marriage as "the nearest thing to the beatific vision we can know. The intense pleasure and delight of the act itself may be like a sword piercing the heart, but though momentary in itself, it colors the hours and days, people and events, before and after, so that one is apt to feel that one is seeing others as God sees them, loving them as God loves them."[29] In the same article, possibly reflecting on her own experience, she lamented the loss of virginity before marriage as a loss of integrity and wholeness. She went on to observe that sex outside of marriage and the reduction of sex to recreation is a reduction of sex to its animal aspects and results in the loss of its spiritual possibilities. For Day, just as sex within the proper order can approach the beatific vision, the misuse of sex can descend into the blackness of hell. About the sexual revolution she wrote:

> And in these days when all the senses are indulged and catered to, there is a living on the surface, a surface excitement, a titillation which never goes below to the great depths of passion. Even Catholics are affected by these attitudes toward sex. They indulge all the pleasures of the day. Music is savage, stirring the blood, movements of the dance are provocative, dress is immodest, pictures are suggestive.
>
> When sex is used it takes on the quality of the demonic, and to descend into the blackness is to have a foretaste of hell "where no order is but everlasting horror dwelleth" [Job 10:22].[30]

[29] Dorothy Day, "Reflections during Advent", pt. 3, "Chastity", *Ave Maria*, December 10, 1966, Catholic Worker Movement website, http://www.catholicworker.org/dorothyday/articles/561.html.

[30] Quoted in William D. Miller, *All Is Grace: The Spirituality of Dorothy Day* (Garden City, N.Y.: Doubleday, 1987), 164.

Day strongly supported the Church's teachings on contraception and abortion. In an article from 1972 she compares birth control and abortion to genocide.[31] And in a 1973 letter to *Commonweal*, she wrote: "Thank God we have a Pope Paul who upholds *respect for life*, an ideal so lofty, so high, so important even when it seems he has the whole Catholic world against him."[32] But even much earlier, before these issues became divisive inside and outside the Church, Day was clear in her opposition to both practices. In 1948 she observed: "The prevention of conception when the act one is performing is for the purpose of fusing the two lives more closely and so enrich them that another life springs forth; aborting of a life conceived—these sins are great frustrations in the natural and spiritual order."[33]

In the fifties and sixties she also criticized U.S. foreign policy when it did not do more to oppose the practice of abortion as a means of birth control in other countries.[34] She also maintained that birth control and abortion are harmful to women: "Sex is a gigantic force in our lives and unless controlled becomes unbridled lust under which woman is victim and suffers most of all. When man takes to himself the right to use sex for pleasure alone, cutting

[31] Dorothy Day, "On Pilgrimage—December 1972", *Catholic Worker*, December 1972, Catholic Worker Movement website, http://www.catholic worker.org/dorothyday/articles/526.html.

[32] Dorothy Day to the editors of *Commonweal*, August 20, 1973, in *All the Way to Heaven*, 405. Emphasis in original.

[33] Dorothy Day, *On Pilgrimage* (Grand Rapids, Mich.: Wm. B. Eerdmans, 1999), 228.

[34] See, for example, Dorothy Day, "Theophane Venard and Ho Chi Minh", *Catholic Worker*, May 1954, Catholic Worker Movement website, http://www .catholicworker.org/dorothyday/articles/667.html, and "On Pilgrimage—December 1961", *Catholic Worker*, December 1961, Catholic Worker Movement website, http://www.catholicworker.org/dorothyday/articles/788.html.

it away from its creative aspect by artificial birth control, by perverse practices, he is denying 'The Absolute Supremacy of the Creative Deity.' "[35] Day's commitment to the poor and to peace was bound up with her commitment to the sanctity of all human life, and she extended this to the unborn. She wrote to Thomas Merton that she was troubled by the hypocrisy she witnessed when "those in this peace crowd do not hesitate to have abortions."[36] She wrote in a similar vein to Jim Forest: "To me sex is important, not just a plaything, a pleasure. By our sexuality we are co-creators in a most real sense. Here we are as pacifists seemingly on the side of life, and so many in the peace movement denying life."[37]

In 1974 Day's was one of seven signatures on the Catholic Peace Fellowship's Statement on Abortion criticizing the Supreme Court's decision in *Roe v. Wade*. The letter stated:

> We reject categorically the Supreme Court's argument that abortion is an exclusively private matter to be decided by the prospective mother and her physician. We protest the thoroughly logical and perhaps inevitable extension of a practice which, though first argued in a personal context, has rapidly become a social policy involving publicly funded clinics and supportive agencies.
>
> This is not a "Catholic issue," and to dismiss it as such is to deny the dedication and the contribution of those of other religions and of none. Nor is it simply a matter of one group of citizens imposing its own morality upon others, any more so than our conscientious resistance to the war in

[35] Miller, *All Is Grace*, 165–66.

[36] Dorothy Day to Thomas Merton, November 12, 1962, in *All the Way to Heaven*, 289.

[37] Dorothy Day to Jim Forest, March 3, 1967, in *All the Way to Heaven*, 333.

Viet Nam, to conscription etc. Indeed we insist that these positions are all of one piece, stemming from what Albert Schweitzer called, "reverence for life," and the consequent obligation to oppose any policy or practice which would give one human being the right to determine whether or not another shall be permitted to live.[38]

Finally, Alice Lange shared an account of her experience with Dorothy Day that demonstrates her opposition to abortion. Lange met Day in May 1971 when Day had been invited to give a talk on women's rights at South Dakota State College. As Lange recalled:

The young woman in charge of the meeting welcomed the audience and gave a short background on Dorothy Day in preparation for Dorothy's presentation. She announced that Miss Day understood a woman's right to choose, and that abortion was very much at the heart of empowering women. Dorothy, who was sitting in the front row, rose out of her chair to her full angular forbidding height, shook her finger at the speaker, and angrily scolded her on the falseness of such a belief, on the dignity of women and the child's right to life.... After her lecture there was nothing more to say. The young women hung their heads and were silent. We picked up our handbags and left.[39]

Day's own youthful experience of sexual activity, betrayal, and abortion led her to see firsthand the wisdom of the Church's teachings on these matters. She was known to exhort the young people around her, particularly women, not to make the same mistakes she did.

The Influence of Her Contemporaries

The last aspect of Day's spirituality to consider is the influence of her friends and spiritual directors. We have already discussed the extent to which Peter Maurin influenced Day; two other important influences were Father Virgil Michel, O.S.B. (1890–1938), and Father John Hugo (1911–1985).

Father Virgil Michel was a Benedictine priest from Saint John's Abbey in Collegeville, Minnesota. Like Peter Maurin, he was very interested in the philosophy of personalism. Father Michel was also one of the leaders in the United States of what is referred to as the Liturgical Movement, which sought to change Roman Catholic liturgies in order to make them more accessible to the laity and to promote more lay participation. The movement advocated changes such as lay participation in liturgical music, Mass in the vernacular instead of Latin, and greater numbers of the lay faithful receiving Communion. The Liturgical Movement also encouraged the laity to pray the daily Office as a way of drawing them beyond their private prayers and into the common prayer life of the Church.

Father Michel wanted the laity to have a deeper sense of their unity in the Church. He saw this as an essential aspect of the doctrine of the mystical body of Christ. He maintained:

> The traditional Christian conception of our supernatural life is that of the life of a fellowship of souls known as the mystical body of Christ. All members united to Christ are

intimately united with each other in Christ.... Each individual member is responsible for his share in maintaining
the supernatural life of the entire mystical body; each one
has the duty, as far as circumstances allow, to come to the
help of his fellow members, and thus to maintain the common life of the entire body.[40]

Drawing from Saint Paul's First Letter to the Corinthi-
ans, Father Michel emphasized that all of the baptized are
members of the same mystical body. As Saint Paul wrote:
"For just as the body is one and has many members, and
all the members of the body, though many, are one body,
so it is with Christ. For by one Spirit we were all baptized
into one body—Jews or Greeks, slaves or free—and all
were made to drink of one Spirit.... Now you are the
body of Christ and individually members of it" (1 Cor
12:12–13, 27).

Day first came in contact with Father Michel in 1933,
and they became friends. Day was already attending daily
Mass, and through Father Michel she began to see more
clearly the connection between daily Mass and the reception of the sacraments, and her work in the Catholic
Worker movement. The teachings on the mystical body
of Christ helped her to formulate her own theory of one's
relationship and responsibility to the poor. In the January
1936 edition of the *Catholic Worker*, Day wrote about the
connection between the Liturgical Movement and service
to the poor:

When we recite prime and compline we are using the
inspired prayer of the church. When we pray with Christ
(not to him) we realize Christ as our Brother. We think

[40] Virgil Michel, *Christian Social Construction* (Milwaukee, Wis.: Bruce, 1937), 7.

of all men as brothers then, as members of the Mystical Body of Christ. "We are all members, one of another," and, remembering this, we can never be indifferent to the social miseries and evils of the day. The dogma of the Mystical Body has tremendous social implications.[41]

She added that through the prayer of the Church "we find that it is now not us but Christ in us, who is working to combat injustice and oppression. We are on our way to becoming 'other Christs.' We cannot build up the idea of the apostolate of the laity without the foundation of the liturgy."

Under Father Michel's influence Day had begun the practice of communal prayer of the Office and emphasized to the Catholic Worker volunteers the importance of daily Mass (being a Benedictine, Father Michel was one of the priests who introduced Day to the teachings of Saint Benedict on work and prayer discussed in chapter 4). Day embraced participating in the Mass and receiving the Eucharist as physically reinforcing the unity among the baptized. She frequently observed that since all persons are members or potential members of the body of Christ, all members of society must be treated with the care and the respect we would show to Christ.

Along with Father Michel and the Liturgical Movement, influences on Day's spirituality included, in her later years, her experience of the Lacouture retreats. In the first part of the twentieth century, the Church placed renewed emphasis on the importance of spiritual retreats not only for priests and religious but also for the laity. One significant retreat experience that arose at this time was

---

[41] Dorothy Day, "Liturgy and Sociology", *Catholic Worker*, January 1936, Catholic Worker Movement website, http://www.catholicworker.org /dorothyday/articles/296.html.

based upon the retreats offered by the Canadian Jesuit priest Father Onesimus Lacouture (1881–1951). Father Lacouture modeled his retreats on the spiritual exercises of Saint Ignatius Loyola. They were designed as a four-week program that focused on the purification of heart and spirit, union with Christ, and docility to the Holy Spirit.[42] The retreat was designed such that a person could attend one week at a time rather than four weeks in a row. Day, whose previous experience of retreats had not been positive, became aware of the Lacouture retreat in 1940 and was encouraged to make the retreat with Father John Hugo, a priest in the Diocese of Pittsburgh. In July 1941 Day traveled to Oakmont, Pennsylvania, to partici-pate in a week of retreat with Father Hugo. Here is how she described it: "The five days of complete silence during the retreat were a feast indeed. Every day we had four conferences of an hour each, and after each conference we went to the chapel to pray. Fr. Hugo was a brilliant teacher and one could see he was taking great joy in his work."[43] Day was overwhelmed with the message, beauty, and experience of the retreat, and she was to repeat it more than twenty times in her life. Day described the joy she experienced on the retreat: "This is what I was looking for in explanation of Christian life. . . . I saw things as a whole for the first time with a delight, a joy, an excitement which is hard to describe. This is what I expected when I became a Catholic."[44] Father Hugo became an important spiritual adviser to Day. She also recommended the retreat to oth-ers in the Catholic Worker movement and to the readers

[42] Brigid O'Shea Merriman, *Searching for Christ: The Spirituality of Dorothy Day* (Notre Dame, Ind.: University of Notre Dame Press, 1994), 133.

[43] Day, *Long Loneliness*, 255.

[44] Quoted in Jim Forest, *Love Is the Measure: A Biography of Dorothy Day* (Maryknoll, N.Y.: Orbis Books, 1986), 83.

of the newspaper. The Catholic Worker houses and farms soon became centers for Lacouture retreats.

The emphasis of the retreats was the Gospel message of faith and love. The retreats called people to evaluate their lives, discovering the extent to which the love of God was at the center of everything they did. Retreatants discovered that those things that were not done for the love of God should be abandoned. As Day maintained: "If people did not go away from the retreat examining their consciences as to the work they did in the world, their material goods, their attachments, then it was a failure. Such a retreat should be like a shock treatment, we thought, putting the 'old man' to death, bringing us to new life."[45] As we have seen before, Day was always interested in how she could synthesize her faith with her work, and the retreats offered her not only a deeper understanding of her faith but also an important aid to living it out.[46] The retreats confirmed her commitment to the poor and to a life of voluntary poverty.

But the retreats were not without controversy. Many people thought they promoted an overemphasis on penance and an overscrupulous examination of one's attachments. Some interpreted the retreats' harsh evaluation of physical pleasures such as smoking or listening to the radio—because they reflected a love for things other than God—as promoting a hatred of the body. Because of these concerns, several bishops forbade the retreats in their dioceses. For a time Father Hugo was not allowed to offer the retreats anywhere, and the Jesuits forbade Father Lacouture from offering them. While Day for the most part avoided getting involved in the controversies, she never

[45] Day, *Long Loneliness*, 259.
[46] Merriman, *Searching for Christ*, 163.

ceased promoting the retreats and attending them; they clearly provided her with needed spiritual nourishment. As she wrote: "It is not only for others that I must have these retreats. It is because I too am hungry and thirsty for the bread of the strong. I too must nourish myself to do the work I have undertaken; I too must drink at these good springs so that I may not be an empty cistern and unable to help others."[47]

Dorothy Day had a rich and varied spirituality that drew from several sources: Scripture, the lives of the saints, the teaching of the Church, and her contemporaries. In the next chapters we will explore how she brought this spirituality to fruition in her life as the leader of the Catholic Worker movement.

[47] Day, *Long Loneliness*, 263.

Chapter Six

THE WORKS OF MERCY

The works of mercy are central to the mission of the Catholic Worker movement. Dorothy Day devoted her life to the daily performance of these works. According to the *Catechism of the Catholic Church*, "The *works of mercy* are charitable actions by which we come to the aid of our neighbor in his spiritual and bodily necessities."[1] As such, the works of mercy are directed to our neighbor's whole being, body and soul. Church tradition identifies seven corporal works of mercy and seven spiritual works of mercy:

The Corporal Works of Mercy

Feed the hungry
Give drink to the thirsty
Shelter the homeless
Clothe the naked
Visit the sick
Visit the imprisoned
Bury the dead

The Spiritual Works of Mercy

Instruct the ignorant
Counsel the doubtful

---

[1] *CCC* 2447. Emphasis in original.

Admonish the sinner
Comfort the sorrowful
Bear wrongs patiently
Forgive all injuries
Pray for the living and the dead

These works of mercy have their foundation in both Scripture and in Church teachings.

In general, the call to mercy can be found in the Beatitudes: "Blessed are the merciful, for they shall obtain mercy" (Mt 5:7). But one can also find instruction elsewhere in Scripture to perform specific acts of mercy. For example, in Isaiah 58:7 the prophet tells us that God's command for those who would be righteous is "to share your bread with the hungry, and bring the homeless poor into your house; when you see the naked, to cover him, and not to hide yourself from your own flesh". The scriptural foundation of the corporal works can also be seen clearly in the Gospel of Matthew 25:31–46 (see pp. 68–69), in which Jesus tells us that at the last judgment the saved will be separated from the damned based upon whether they fed the hungry, clothed the naked, welcomed the stranger, comforted the sick, and visited the prisoner.

The spiritual works of mercy are also drawn from both Old and New Testament sources. For example, the Old Testament assures us that "as a mother comforts her son, so I will comfort you" (Is 66:13). In the New Testament, the letters of Saint Paul are one source of the spiritual works. For example:

My brothers, if someone is detected in sin, you who live
by the Spirit should gently set him right. (Gal 6:1)
Let the word of Christ, rich as it is, dwell in you. In wisdom made perfect, instruct and admonish one another. (Col 3:16)

Bear with one another; forgive whatever grievances you
   have against one another. Forgive as the Lord has forgiven you. (Col 3:12)

At every opportunity pray in the Spirit, using prayers and
   petitions of every sort. Pray constantly and attentively
   for all in the holy company. (Eph 6:18)

The works of mercy are an important part of the Church's
tradition; the lists of the seven corporal and seven spiritual
works were codified in the medieval period.

To understand the works of mercy correctly, it is important to consider the Church's understanding of mercy. In *The
City of God*, Saint Augustine asked: "Now, what is mercy
but a certain feeling of compassion in our hearts, evoked by
the misery of another and compelling us to offer all possible aid?"[2] Similarly, Saint Thomas Aquinas, in the *Summa
Theologiae*, defined mercy as "grief for another's distress".[3]
Saint Thomas also discussed some important distinctions
to consider regarding mercy. He recognized that we may
respond on an emotional level to the distress of others, and
in this way mercy is experienced as a passion. But mercy
can also result from our rational judgment that someone's
distress ought to be relieved. In this case, for Saint Thomas,
our mercy is not a passion but a virtue. He also emphasized
that mercy is the result of a strong identification of oneself
with the other in that "one grieves or sorrows for another's
distress, in so far as one looks upon another's distress as
one's own."[4] Thus, a work of mercy is not possible if one
attempts to remain detached from the other.

---

[2] Augustine, *The City of God*, bk. 9, chap. 5, trans. Gerald Walsh and Grace
Monahan, Fathers of the Church 24 (New York: Fathers of the Church, 1952),
2:85.

[3] Thomas Aquinas, *Summa Theologiae*, trans. English Dominican Fathers
(New York: Benziger Brothers, 1948), II–II, q. 30, art. 2 (hereafter cited as *ST*).

[4] *ST* II–II, q. 30, art. 2.

The *Catechism of the Catholic Church* also identifies a work of mercy as "a work of justice pleasing to God".[5] This is the sense in which Dorothy Day and Peter Maurin understood the works of mercy. For them, feeding or clothing the poor was as much an act of justice as it was an act of charity. People have a right to eat and to be sheltered. As Saint Gregory the Great said: "When we attend to the needs of those in want, we give them what is theirs, not ours. More than performing works of mercy, we are paying a debt of justice."[6] The works of mercy entail both charity and justice. Thus, to understand these works better, we must also correctly understand the relationship between charity and justice.

Charity and Justice

In the Catholic tradition justice is identified as one of the four cardinal virtues. The *Catechism of the Catholic Church* states: "Justice toward men disposes one to respect the rights of each and to establish in human relationships the harmony that promotes equity with regard to persons and to the common good."[7] Justice is an essential aspect of any well-functioning community. As Pope John Paul II observed: "Justice can reduce differences, eliminate discrimination, and assure the conditions necessary for the respect of personal dignity."[8] But at the same time he

[5] *CCC* 2447.

[6] Gregory the Great, *Book of Pastoral Rule* 3.21, quoted in Pontifical Council for Justice and Peace, *Compendium of the Social Doctrine of the Church* (Washington, D.C.: United States Conference of Catholic Bishops, 2005), 184.

[7] *CCC* 1807.

[8] John Paul II, address to UNIV '99 Congress of University Students, March 30, 1999, no. 3.

recognized: "Justice, however, requires a soul. And the soul of justice is charity, a charity which becomes service of the whole man."[9] In his encyclical *Dives in Misericordia*, Pope John Paul II warned that the pursuit of justice divorced from charity can often result in injustice. He wrote: "The experience of the past and of our own time demonstrates that justice alone is not enough, that it can even lead to the negation and destruction of itself, if that deeper power, which is love, is not allowed to shape human life in its various dimensions."[10]

Charity also must be properly understood to appreciate its relationship to justice. Charity (*caritas*), or love, is one of the theological virtues. Authentic acts of charity are by definition acts of love. As Saint Paul wrote: "If I give everything I have to feed the poor and hand over my body to be burned, but have not love [*caritatem*], I gain nothing" (1 Cor 13:3). But our common use of the word *charity* is often missing this sense of love. As the American bishops observed in 1999: "In recent years, charity has often been perceived negatively. Those who undertake charitable activities are seen as well-meaning 'do-gooders' who actually foster dependency. Those who receive charity are treated in a demeaning manner. Even the word 'charity' has been transformed by some into a derogatory term."[11] In *The Long Loneliness*, even Day described charity as "a word to choke over" if it did not recognize "man's dignity and worth, and what was due to him in justice".[12] True charity should not be confused with mere "do-gooder" activities.

[9] Ibid.

[10] John Paul II, *Dives in Misericordia* (1980), no. 12.

[11] United States Conference of Catholic Bishops, "In All Things Charity: A Pastoral Challenge for the New Millennium" (November 18, 1999), 3.17.

[12] Dorothy Day, *The Long Loneliness* (New York: Harper and Brothers, 1952), 150.

Saint Thomas Aquinas explained the difference by emphasizing that charity is more than just goodwill toward another. He points out that in an act of goodwill, we might do something for the good of other persons and want the best for them, but if we do not feel united to them, if we remain detached, this is not yet authentic charity. For Saint Thomas, true charity "denotes a certain union of affections between the lover and the beloved, in as much as the lover deems the beloved as somewhat united to him, or belonging to him, and so tends toward him".[13] In *Deus Caritas Est*, Pope Benedict XVI echoed this truth: "My deep personal sharing in the needs and suffering of others becomes a sharing of my very self with them: if my gift is not to prove a source of humiliation, I must give to others not only something that is my own, but my very self; I must be personally present in my gift."[14] Similarly, Dorothy Day was fond of quoting the rather paradoxical line from Saint Vincent de Paul: "It is only by feeling your love that the poor will forgive you for the gifts of bread."[15] What Pope Benedict and Saint Vincent de Paul recognized is that an act of "charity" without love can often be demeaning to the person who receives it. But when the act is done out of love for the other, then the other's dignity is preserved and charity can be accepted. At the start of the new millennium, Pope John Paul II observed: "Now is the time for a new 'creativity' in charity, not only by ensuring that help is effective but also by 'getting close' to those who suffer, so that the hand that helps is seen not as a humiliating handout but as a sharing

[13] *ST* II–II, q. 27, art. 2.

[14] Benedict XVI, *Deus Caritas Est: On Christian Love* (2005), no. 34.

[15] See, for example, Dorothy Day, "On Pilgrimage", *Catholic Worker*, January 1959, Catholic Worker Movement website, http://www.catholicworker.org/dorothyday/articles/178.html.

between brothers and sisters."[16] Thus, true charity must be done out of love for and unity with the other.

This relationship between charity and justice is also reflected in the Church's teachings regarding the "preferential option for the poor". The United States Conference of Catholic Bishops has summarized the preferential option this way: "Our tradition calls us to put the needs of the poor and the vulnerable first. As Christians, we are called to respond to the needs of all our sisters and brothers, but those with the greatest needs require the greatest response."[17] As Pope Francis has observed: "Each individual Christian and every community is called to be an instrument of God for the liberation and promotion of the poor, and for enabling them to be fully a part of society."[18] Pope John Paul II used the phrase "love of preference for the poor", which means giving a "primacy in the exercise of Christian charity" to those whose needs are the greatest.[19] Since their needs are for the basic goods (life, food, shelter, etc.) to which all have a right, this option entails both charity and justice. In his encyclical letter *Centesimus Annus: On the Hundredth Anniversary of "Rerum Novarum"*, Pope John Paul II warned us:

> But it will be necessary above all to abandon a mentality in which the poor—as individuals and as peoples—are considered a burden, as irksome intruders trying to consume what others have produced. The poor ask for the right to

[16] John Paul II, *Novo Millennio Ineunte: At the Close of the Great Jubilee of the Year 2000* (2001), no. 50.

[17] United States Conference of Catholic Bishops, *A Century of Social Teaching: A Common Heritage, a Continuing Challenge* (Washington, D.C.: United States Catholic Conference, 1990), 6–7.

[18] Francis, *Evangelii Gaudium* (2013), no. 187.

[19] John Paul II, *Sollicitudo Rei Socialis* (1987), no. 42.

share in enjoying material goods and to make good use of their capacity for work, thus creating a world that is more just and prosperous for all.[20]

Pope Francis also wrote that the poor need not just material care but spiritual care as well: "Our preferential option for the poor must mainly translate into a privileged and preferential religious care."[21]

The American bishops have recognized a connection between our treatment of the poor and the promotion of a culture of death: "Frequently, people are tempted to blame the poor for the conditions that oppress them.... Such a mentality plagues our present times leading to a culture of death, which includes abortion, infanticide, euthanasia, assisted suicide, and capital punishment."[22]

To help maintain the Christian understanding of the poor as our brothers, it is important to appreciate this relationship between charity and justice. To again quote what the bishops have said: "One cannot ignore the demands of either charity or justice in the practice of our faith. Our Catholic teaching and tradition tell us that both of these virtues are complementary, inter-dependent, and divinely inspired."[23]

Works of Mercy in Practice

When Peter Maurin first approached Dorothy Day to join him in founding what was to become the Catholic

---

[20] John Paul II, *Centesimus Annus: On the Hundredth Anniversary of "Rerum Novarum"* (1991), no. 28.

[21] Francis, *Evangelii Gaudium*, no. 200.

[22] United States Conference of Catholic Bishops, "In All Things Charity", 3.16.

[23] Ibid.

Worker movement, he proposed a project aimed at real-izing the Gospel message in contemporary society. At the heart of his project was an active life of the works of mercy through three distinct endeavors: (1) the publication of a newspaper and opportunities for roundtable discussions to bring the social teachings of the Church to the man in the street, (2) the establishment of houses of hospitality and the practice of voluntary poverty, and (3) the establishment of farming communes to provide food and work for the unemployed.[24] Taken together, these three pursuits allow for both the corporal and the spiritual acts of mercy to be put into practice.

The Newspaper

The first edition of the *Catholic Worker*, published on May 1, 1933, included one of Peter Maurin's Easy Essays, "Blowing the Dynamite", which says in part:

> To blow the dynamite
> of a message
> is the only way
> to make that message
> dynamic.
>
> Catholic scholars
> have taken the dynamite
> of the church;
> they have wrapped it up
> in nice phraseology,
> have placed it
> in an hermetically

[24] Dorothy Day, *Peter Maurin: Apostle to the World*, with Francis J. Sicius (Maryknoll, N.Y.: Orbis Books, 2004), 51.

sealed container,
and sat on the lid.

It is about time
to take the lid off
and to make
the Catholic dynamite
dynamic.[25]

The "dynamite" Maurin wanted to "blow" is the teaching on social issues contained in the Gospels, the lives of the saints, and the Church's tradition. Maurin thought that people in general, and Catholics in particular, were ignorant of the rich history of social teaching of the Church and that the Church itself was guilty of failing to catechize the faithful on these topics. Thus, the newspaper, the *Catholic Worker*, was to perform four of the spiritual works of mercy: instruct the ignorant, counsel the doubtful, comfort the sorrowful, and admonish the sinner.[26] And it was this newspaper work that initially appealed to Dorothy Day. She recounted: "But of course it was getting out a labor paper which caught my imagination, popularizing the teachings of the Church in regard to social matters, bringing the man in the street a Christian solution of unemployment, a way of rebuilding the social order."[27] Day published the first edition out of her apartment but was soon able to rent a vacant barbershop to serve as the newspaper office. Using a donated desk and typewriter,

[25] Ibid., 143–44.

[26] Dorothy Day, "Letter to Our Readers at the Beginning of Our Fifteenth Year", *Catholic Worker*, May 1947, Catholic Worker Movement website, http://www.catholicworker.org/dorothyday/articles/155.html.

[27] Dorothy Day, *House of Hospitality* (New York: Sheed and Ward, 1939), xxvii.

the paper was produced and published on a monthly basis. Along with producing the paper, the office served as a neighborhood center where Maurin could invite speakers and engage people in what he called "round-table discussions for the clarification of thought" regarding the Church's teachings. Visitors included Jacques Maritain and Hilaire Belloc. The office also became a center for helping the poor of the neighborhood to find shelter and clothing.

Houses of Hospitality

In the September 1933 issue of the *Catholic Worker*, Peter Maurin wrote an open letter to the U.S. bishops talking about the tradition of hospices in the medieval Church. These hospices, or houses of hospitality, were places where the sick, the poor, the orphaned, and the old could be cared for. Maurin urged that the practice be renewed with houses of hospitality open in every diocese and even every parish. These houses could serve not only as shelters but as places for prayer, discussion, and study. A woman who read Maurin's letter came to the editorial office and spoke to Day about the need for this type of hospice for women who had been evicted and were now homeless. Day was able to locate a six-room apartment that could accommodate fifteen beds. The rent was fifty dollars a month, and the local parish helped raise the money. Donors included a group of young working women who pledged twenty-five cents per week from their small wages to help pay the cost. Within a year, Day was able to locate a three-story, eleven-room tenement house that could accommodate both women and men as well as provide office space for the paper. Day, Maurin, and the other volunteers shared this house with their "guests". Though the locations changed over the years, Day lived the rest of her life in these houses of hospitality, usually sharing a room with a guest. A typical house was home to twenty-five to thirty-five people. And though not part of the initial plan, it quickly became the case that during the day these houses also served as soup kitchens for the poor and the unemployed, serving hundreds of people each day. Others attracted to the Catholic Worker movement soon opened similar houses across the country.

It was in these houses of hospitality that Day and the others most directly engaged in the corporal works of mercy: feeding the hungry, clothing the naked, giving shelter to the homeless, and taking care of the sick. In 1939 Day wrote an article describing the shared life in the houses of hospitality. She emphasized the commitment to small communities rather than large institutions: "We believe it is most necessary to give a sense of family life to those who come to us. We believe a sense of security is as necessary as bread or shelter." Further, she explained: "There are all nationalities among us and all ages, from eighteen to seventy-two. Some have been with us for five years and probably will die with us. Some are with us for only a few months and then find jobs and leave and make room for others. Many are unemployable and we must take care of them as we would a member of the family who cannot find work."[28] All in the house were expected to share in the work according to their abilities and to share in the common spiritual life of the house. The deep sense of the houses of hospitality as an experience of family reveals the extent to which they reflect the notion of

<hr />

[28] Dorothy Day, "House of Hospitality", *Catholic Worker*, May 1939, Catholic Worker Movement website, http://www.catholicworker.org/dorothyday /articles/342.html.

charity discussed above. By living in voluntary poverty with the guests, the workers shared in their lives, and so works of mercy were accepted as one accepts the kindness of a family member, which is with gratitude and no sense of being demeaned.

Day was quick to acknowledge that life in the houses of hospitality was not easy, and she never sought to romanticize it. Such situations provide ample opportunity for bearing wrongs patiently and forgiving offenses. She found that unmarried volunteers usually found it easier than those who were married and in some instances trying to raise a family in this situation. Day experienced firsthand the difficulties of raising her own daughter, Tamar, in a house of hospitality. The guests in the house demanded much of Day's time, and she often feared that she was neglecting Tamar. And there were instances of guests stealing or destroying her daughter's things.[29] In a 1948 article in the paper, Day again described life in a house of hospitality. When one of the workers read the piece, she asked Day to add the following:

> Remind the people that such work is monotonous.... We all talk about *the little way*, and mothers especially know how one meal follows another, and daily there is washing, and the house to pick up, and the wild romantic glamour of married life soon fades to give place to something deeper. It is the same with the work. People come in all of a glow to help the poor, and their very compassion makes them think there must be some quicker way to serve them; make laws, change conditions, get better housing, working conditions, racial justice, etc. But the immediate work remains, the works of mercy, and there are few to do them. Perseverance, endurance, faithfulness

[29] Day, *Long Loneliness*, 237.

to the poor—we should be wedded to Lady Poverty as St. Francis was—these are the things to stress.[30]

For Day and the others in the Catholic Worker movement, it was in the concrete performance of each daily task that the works of mercy were actualized. Currently, there are more than 180 Catholic Worker houses across the United States and around the world.

Farming Communities

The third aspect of Peter Maurin's project was the establishment of farming communities. He was convinced that farming communities were an essential part of the distributist approach to economics. Long before the term "green revolution" was popular, Peter Maurin used it (as opposed to the communist "red revolution") to describe the development of farming communities that could be a self-sufficient response to the growing agriculture industry. He also pointed out that there was no unemployment on a farm, that all could contribute to the work. So after establishing the newspaper and the house of hospitality, in the spring of 1935 the Catholic Worker established its first small farm on Staten Island. The people living on the farm raised all the vegetables they needed for themselves plus supplied the house of hospitality in the city with vegetables for the soup kitchen. Soon another, larger farm was acquired in Easton, Pennsylvania, and this farm was later replaced by one in New York.[31] Day often split her time

---

[30] Dorothy Day, "Letter on Hospices", *Catholic Worker*, January 1948, Catholic Worker Movement website, http://www.catholicworker.org/dorothy day/articles/183.html. Emphasis in original.

[31] For a detailed account of the farming communities, see Dorothy Day, *Loaves and Fishes* (Maryknoll, N.Y.: Orbis Books, 1997), chap. 4.

between the house of hospitality in the city and the farms, though she admitted that she and other city dwellers made "ridiculous" farmers. The farms also served as rural houses of hospitality and as retreat centers. In other words, like the urban houses of hospitality, they were centers for performing the spiritual and corporal works of mercy. Though not as prolific as the houses of hospitality, today nearly two dozen Catholic Worker farms are in operation around the United States.[32]

Concern for the Dead

Both the corporal and spiritual works of mercy include acts on behalf of the dead. Day was always concerned with the proper burial of the dead and the saying of prayers for them. Over the years, Day witnessed the death of many volunteers and guests at the houses of hospitality, even of men as they stood in the breadlines. She made sure they received the last rites, a funeral Mass, and a proper burial. In a November 1953 article, Day mentioned the names of dead kept on a list in her missal so that she could pray for them every day. The list is quite long. In 1927 she wrote, shortly after her conversion, that the son of a friend had committed suicide, and she wondered then why one would pray for a person whose life was over. She asked her confessor about this, and he explained: "There is no time with God. All the prayers you will say in the future for this soul will count. God has said, 'ask and ye shall receive.' He has promised this. If you keep asking for God's mercy for that soul, you can be sure your prayers will be

[32] See Eric Anglada, "Taking Root: The History and New Growth of Catholic Worker Farms", *America*, May 6, 2013, 13–15.

answered."[33] Day was comforted by this and made praying for the dead one of her daily works of mercy.

The works of mercy have a long tradition in the Catholic Church. It was through these works that Christians first distinguished themselves. In the third century Tertullian recorded that Roman pagans said of Christians, "See how they love one another." It was the Christian witness embodied in the works of mercy that helped to convert a pagan age. Day and Maurin were convinced that the performance of these works could be as transformative on contemporary culture.

[33] Dorothy Day, "There Is No Time with God", *Catholic Worker*, November 1953, Catholic Worker Movement website, http://www.catholicworker.org/dorothyday/articles/657.html.

Chapter Seven

PEACEMAKER

Dorothy Day's pacifism was perhaps her most controversial position. The Catholic Worker movement preferred the term *peacemaker* to *pacifist* because it reflected an active pursuit of a good.[1] Day's pacifism often put her at odds with American public opinion, leaders in the Catholic Church, and even other members of the Catholic Worker movement. But her strong commitment also helped to shape the contemporary Church's teachings on war.

The Church, since its beginnings, has struggled to reconcile Christ's commandment to love one's enemies and His reference to the blessedness of the peacemakers with the need to respond to injustice with force. Saint Augustine was one of the first Christians to address this issue. The saint found war deplorable, but he allowed that it might be necessary and permissible under certain circumstances. In *The City of God*, he wrote: "A just war ... is justified only by the injustice of an aggressor; and that injustice ought to be a source of grief to any good man, because it

[1] John L. LeBrun, "The Way of Love: Pacifism and the Catholic Worker Movement, 1933–1939", in *Dorothy Day and the Catholic Worker Movement: Centenary Essays*, ed. William Thorn, Phillip Runkel, and Susan Mountin (Milwaukee, Wis.: Marquette University Press, 2001), 449.

is a human injustice."[2] Following Saint Augustine, Saint Thomas Aquinas argues in the *Summa Theologiae* that three requirements must be met for a war to be just:

> the authority by whom the war is waged must be legitimate (for Saint Thomas the legitimate authority would be a ruler who was entrusted with overseeing the common good);
> the cause one is fighting for must be just; and
> the one waging war must intend it to advance good and to prevent evil.[3]

Thus, a just war was understood to be one that sought to stop unjust aggression by one state against another and to reestablish peace. In this sense a just war was viewed as a form of self-defense or the defense of a weaker party who was being unjustly attacked by an aggressor.

Over the years, changes in the understanding of human rights and national identity, along with changes in how wars are waged, have resulted in additional requirements in just war theory. The *Catechism of the Catholic Church* stipulates four conditions that must be met in order for a war to be recognized as just:

> the damage inflicted by the aggressor on the nation or community of nations must be lasting, grave, and certain;
> all other means of putting an end to [the aggression] must have been shown to be impractical or ineffective;
> there must be serious prospects of success;

---

[2] Augustine, *The City of God*, bk. 19, chap. 17, trans. Gerald Walsh and Daniel Honan, Fathers of the Church 24 (New York: Fathers of the Church, 1952), 3:207.

[3] *ST* II–II, q. 40, art. 1.

the use of arms must not produce evils and disorders graver than the evil to be eliminated. The power of modern means of destruction weighs very heavily in evaluating this condition.[4]

These basic precepts of just war theory are intended not as a checklist but as a guide in the prudential moral reasoning that always must be at work when countries consider waging war.

These criteria concern primarily the decision to go to war. But the Church also maintains that there are moral constraints on the waging of war. The *Catechism* says, "the Church and human reason both assert the permanent validity of the *moral law during armed conflict*".[5] And the Vatican II document *Gaudium et Spes* explicitly states that "[t]he mere fact that war has unhappily begun mean that all is fair between the warring parties".[6] The two most important criteria with regard to the waging of war are the immunity of non-combatants and proportionality. Concerning non-combatants, the just war theory maintains that "a state of war only permits the application of force against those actively threatening the innocent."[7] Thus morality demands that one does not kill non-combatants, and this immunity also extends to prisoners of war and the wounded. Proportionality requires that no more force be used than is necessary to meet the military objective.

In recent years the Church has been a strong voice in the condemnation of war and the recognition of the value

[4] *CCC* 2309.

[5] *CCC* 2312. Emphasis in original.

[6] Vatican Council II, Pastoral Constitution on the Church in the Modern World, *Gaudium et Spes* (December 7, 1965), no. 79

[7] *New Catholic Encyclopedia*, 2nd ed., s.v "War, Morality of" (Detroit, Mich.: Thomas Gale, 2003).

of peace. As the *Catechism* maintains: "Respect for and development of human life require *peace*."[8] So in many ways the opposition to war can be understood as part of the Gospel of Life in that peace is a good to be pursued out of respect for human life. But the Church still maintains that in the establishment of peace, the use of force may be necessary. As recently as November 2015, in light of terrorist attacks in Paris, the Vatican affirmed that "those who legitimately hold authority also have the right to use arms to repel aggressors against the civil community entrusted to their responsibility."[9] According to the *Compendium of the Social Doctrine of the Church*:

> *The requirements of legitimate defense justify the existence in States of armed forces, the activity of which should be at the service of peace. Those who defend the security and freedom of a country, in such a spirit, make an authentic contribution to peace.* Everyone who serves in the armed forces is concretely called to defend good, truth and justice in the world. Many are those who, in such circumstances, have sacrificed their lives for these values and in defense of innocent lives.[10]

Finally, the Church recognizes that one can be required to serve in the military because a legitimate authority has "the right and duty to impose on citizens the *obligations necessary for national defense*".[11] But the Church also recognizes the moral legitimacy of a conscientious objector

[8] *CCC* 2304.

[9] Inés San Martín, "Top Vatican Diplomat Backs Use of Force in Wake of Paris Attacks", *Crux*, November 16, 2015, https://cruxnow.com/church/2015/11/16/top-vatican-diplomat-backs-use-of-force-in-wake-of-paris-attacks/

[10] Pontifical Council for Justice and Peace, *Compendium of the Social Doctrine of the Church* (Washington, D.C.: United States Conference of Catholic Bishops, 2005), no. 502. Emphasis in original.

[11] *CCC* 2310. Emphasis in original.

(CO) refusing military service. As the *Catechism* states: "Public authorities should make equitable provision for those who for reasons of conscience refuse to bear arms; these are nonetheless obliged to serve the human community in some other way."[12]

Dorothy Day understood well the Church's teaching on just war theory. Her own pacifism is a position that developed over time. As a young woman, prior to her conversion, Day opposed the United States' entrance into the First World War. But her opposition to World War I was grounded primarily in a communist political view that the war was driven by economic interests that sent the members of the working class of the world to kill each other in order to protect the interests of the bourgeois. For this reason she held that this particular war was unjust. Eventually, Day embraced absolute pacifism as she came to see all war as at odds with the teachings of Jesus Christ, who called the peacemakers blessed and rebuked Peter for taking up the sword.

In December 1936, Day wrote: "The Catholic Worker does not condemn any and all war, but believes the conditions necessary for a 'just war' will not be fulfilled today."[13] The paper published articles by those who identified themselves as "just war pacifists"—that is, those who accepted the teachings on just war but thought that modern warfare, particularly killing of non-combatants, eliminates the possibility of a just war.[14] There is no doubt that Day herself struggled with the demands of pacifism. As she writes in

[12] *CCC* 2311.

[13] Dorothy Day, "For the New Reader", *Catholic Worker*, December 1936, Catholic Worker Movement website, http://www.catholicworker.org/dorothy day/articles/310.html.

[14] See Mark Zwick and Louise Zwick, *The Catholic Worker Movement: Intellectual and Spiritual Origins* (New York: Paulist Press, 2005), 256–57.

The Long Loneliness: "Can there be a just war? Can the conditions laid down by St. Thomas ever be fulfilled? . . . What does God want me to do? And what am I capable of doing? Can I stand out against state and Church? Is it pride, presumption, to think I have the spiritual capacity to use spiritual weapons in the face of the most gigantic tyranny the world has ever seen? Am I capable of suffering, facing martyrdom?"[15] But as Day grew older she did fully embrace an absolute pacifist position committed to non-violence and thus rejecting the just war theory. Day's direct references to just war theory are few, and this might be because she wanted to avoid explicitly opposing the teachings of the Church. But, for example, in 1969, she writes: "But how can we show our love by war, by the extermination of our enemies? If we are followers of Christ, there is no room for speaking of the 'just war.'"[16] Day was aware that in taking this position she was dissenting from Church teaching, but she arrived at her position based upon theological principles and a well-formed conscience.

Day's position was based primarily on two Catholic principles. First is the teaching that all human beings are members or potential members of the mystical body of Christ.[17] This teaching helped Day to see all those around her, particularly the weak and the poor, as united in the mystical body. This teaching also led her to see violence against any member of the human community as violence against Christ and against oneself. Day was fond of quoting

[15] Dorothy Day, *The Long Loneliness* (New York: Harper and Brothers, 1952), 272–73.

[16] Dorothy Day, "On Pilgrimage—February 1969", *Catholic Worker*, February 1969, Catholic Worker Movement website, http://www.catholicworker.org/dorothyday/articles/894.html.

[17] See William T. Cavanaugh, "Dorothy Day and the Mystical Body of Christ in the Second World War", in *Centenary Essays*, 457–64.

Saint Cyprian, who called war "the rending of the Mystical Body of Christ".[18]

The second teaching that shaped Day's pacifism concerns "the counsels of perfection", sometimes called "the evangelical counsels". In the Catholic tradition, the counsels of perfection refer to those teachings of Christ that are "counsels for those who desired to do more than the minimum and to aim at Christian perfection, so far as that can be obtained here upon earth".[19] According to Saint Thomas Aquinas, "the difference between a counsel and a commandment is that the commandment implies obligation, whereas a counsel is left to the option of the one to whom it is given."[20] An example is found in Matthew 19, when the wealthy young man asks Christ how he can gain everlasting life. Christ replies that he should keep the commandments, indicating the minimum he must do. The young man replies that he has done this and wants to know what more he can do. Christ tells him, "If you seek perfection, go, sell your possessions, and give to the poor. You will then have treasure in heaven. Afterward, come back and follow me" (Mt 19:21). This second instruction is the counsel of perfection. Traditionally, the counsels of perfection are identified as poverty, chastity, and obedience. These are often identified with the religious life, but these perfections can be practiced by anyone in a way that is appropriate to his state of life. Saint Thomas Aquinas recognizes the practice of nonviolence as a form of the counsel of obedience: "When a man follows not his will as

---

[18] See, for example, Dorothy Day, "Beyond Politics", *Catholic Worker*, November 1949, Catholic Worker Movement website, http://www.catholic worker.org/dorothyday/articles/166.html.

[19] *Catholic Encyclopedia*, s.v. "Evangelical Counsels", http://www/catholic .org/encyclopedia/view.php?id=3443.

[20] *ST* I–II, q. 108, art. 4.

to some deed which he might do lawfully, he follows the
counsel in that particular case: for instance, if he do good
to his enemies when he is not bound to, or forgive an
injury of which he might justly seek to be avenged."[21] In
this case one is obedient to the Gospel message of loving
one's enemies even though one has been wronged. Thus,
in following the counsels, one who is wronged acknowl-
edges that the other's actions are unjust but remains committed nevertheless to turning the other cheek.

When Day applied the distinction between the minimum obligation and the counsels of perfection, abid-
ing by the criteria of just war theory can be seen as the
minimum a Christian should do, while the practice of
nonviolence is to seek perfection as Christ is perfect.[22]
For this reason, Day would publish articles by those who
opposed particular wars as unjust following just war theory, but she herself always took the position that all war
was unjust because she saw it as "the 'better way'—the
way of the Saints".[23] She recognized that she was trying to affect public opinion and maintained that, "if the
press and the public throughout the world do not speak in
terms of the counsels of perfection, who else will?"[24] For
Day, Christian perfection, including Jesus Christ's witness to nonviolence exemplified in His acceptance of the
Cross, is the highest goal for which Christians can strive.
Some might question whether the counsels, "which are
left to the option of the one to whom it is given", can be
used as the basis for public policy. However, the strife that

[21] Ibid.

[22] See LeBrun, "Way of Love", in *Centenary Essays*, 454–55.

[23] Dorothy Day, "Explains CW Stand on Use of Force", *Catholic Worker*,
September 1938, Catholic Worker Movement website, http://www.catholic
worker.org/dorothyday/articles/216.html.

[24] Ibid.

marked the twentieth century allowed Day ample opportunity to bear witness to her pacifism.

The Spanish Civil War

The Spanish Civil War (1936–1939) was the first significant conflict that required Day to make clear the Catholic Worker's commitment to peace. The Spanish Civil War arose out of a complex historical situation with many competing factions. Catholicism had for centuries been the official religion of Spain, and the Church had been an important influence in Spanish government, traditionally supporting the monarchy. In 1931 King Alfonso XIII was forced to leave the country, and a republican form of government was established, known as the Second Republic. The republic was ruled by a coalition government dominated by socialists and moderates who pursued various reforms, including attempts to reduce the influence of the Church in Spanish government and society. Economic difficulties and disagreements about reform led to a significant split between left-wing and right-wing political parties. In the spring of 1936, as violent unrest began to occur, the military leaders feared a political coup by the Left, and in July 1936, under the leadership of General Francisco Franco, the military itself attempted to take over the government. This move split the country between those who supported the republic (the Republicans) and those who supported Franco (the Nationalists). The Republican side was supplied with arms by the Soviet Union and became dominated by communists. Hitler's Germany and Mussolini's Italy helped arm the Nationalist side, and Franco aligned himself with the fascists. As is the nature of civil wars, the fighting was particularly bitter, with many atrocities committed on both sides.

Among these atrocities was the murder of Catholic religious by the Republican forces, mostly during a period known as the Red Terror. Records show that 13 bishops, 4,172 diocesan priests, 2,364 monks, and 283 nuns—a total of 6,832 Catholic clerics and religious—were executed by the Republican side. Churches were burned and sacred sites destroyed. Not surprisingly, such actions led Catholics around the world, including most American Catholics, to support Franco's forces against the Republicans. But Day and the *Catholic Worker* took a pacifist and neutral stand on the war, a position that was hugely unpopular with the American Catholic community: the circulation of the paper dropped from 160,000 to 50,000, and several bishops banned the paper from churches in their diocese.[25] On the other hand, most of the left-wing activists and papers supported the Republican side against the fascist, leading many of Day's old friends to criticize her neutral stand on the war. But despite the criticism from both sides, Day stood by her position and tried to make it clear to her readers. Day argued that the killing of bishops, priests, and nuns was abhorrent, but she refused to accept that the violence of our enemies required that we respond violently. She recognized those killed as martyrs and prayed for their guidance. But Day asked:

> Do you suppose they died saying grimly, "Alright [*sic*]—we accept martyrdom—we will not lift the sword to defend ourselves but the lay troops will avenge us!" This would be martyrdom wasted. Blood spilled in vain. Or rather did they say with St. Stephen, "Father, forgive them," and pray with love for their conversion? And did

[25] Jim Forest, *Love Is the Measure: A Biography of Dorothy Day* (Maryknoll, N.Y.: Orbis Books, 1986), 73.

they not rather pray, when the light of Christ burst upon them, that love would overcome hatred, that men *dying* for faith, rather than *killing* for their faith, would save the world?[26]

As an alternative to the use of force, Day called for the use of the weapons of the spirit—prayer and the sacraments—to overcome injustice. For Day, this was not mere passive resistance, because "love and prayer are not passive but a most active glowing force."[27] And Day refused to pray for the triumph of either communism or fascism. Rather, Day concluded: "We are praying for the Spanish people—all of them brothers in Christ—all of them Temples of the Holy Ghost, all of them members or potential members of the Mystical Body of Christ."[28] The Spanish Civil War ended in April 1939 with Franco's victory. It was a matter of months before World War II began, and Day faced an even more difficult challenge to her pacifism.

World War II

Even before the United States' entrance into the Second World War, there were many different aspects of the country's response to the conflict, which Day compelled to speak out against. The *Catholic Worker* was critical of President Franklin Roosevelt's decision to allow America to become "the arsenal of democracy" and provide arms to the Allied nations.[29] Day and the Catholic Worker movement also made clear their concern for European Jews, protesting

[26] Day, "Explains CW Stand". Emphasis in original.

[27] Ibid.

[28] Ibid.

[29] See Dorothy Day, "Our Stand", *Catholic Worker*, June 1940, Catholic Worker Movement website, http://www.catholicworker.org/dorothyday/articles/360.html.

at the German embassy regarding the treatment of Jews by the Nazis and criticizing the U.S. government for failing to accept more Jewish refugees. In May 1939 Day was one of the founders of the Committee of Catholics to Fight Anti-Semitism. In the summer of 1940 Day testified before the U.S. Senate Committee on Military Affairs, speaking out against the planned enactment of mandatory conscription, the draft of men into the military service.[30]

Prior to the bombing of Pearl Harbor, many Americans took an isolationist stand and wanted to avoid involvement in a European war. Many were also sympathetic to the plight of the Jews, and so the views of the Catholic Worker movement were not problematic. But with the bombing of Pearl Harbor on December 7, 1941, and America's entry into the war, Day's pacifist position put her at odds with the vast majority of her countrymen. As the United States mobilized for war in January 1942, Day wrote:

> We are still pacifists. Our manifesto is the Sermon on the Mount, which means that we will try to be peacemakers. Speaking for many of our conscientious objectors, we will not participate in armed warfare or in making munitions, or by buying government bonds to prosecute the war, or in urging others to these efforts.
>
> But neither will we be carping in our criticism. We love our country and we love our President. We have been the only country in the world where men and women of all nations have taken refuge from oppression.[31]

[30] Excerpts of Day's testimony can be found in Dorothy Day, "C. W.'s Position", *Catholic Worker*, July–August 1940, Catholic Worker Movement website, https://www.catholicworker.org/dorothyday/articles/363.html.

[31] Dorothy Day, "Our Country Passes from Undeclared War to Declared War; We Continue Our Christian Pacifist Stand", *Catholic Worker*, January 1942, Catholic Worker Movement website, http://www.catholicworker.org/dorothyday/articles/868.html.

Day encouraged all the men associated with the Catholic Worker to file as COs in order to avoid military service. But the movement itself was split between those who supported the war effort and those who continued with a pacifist position. Some houses of hospitality, in different parts of the country, shut down as the workers either volunteered for military service or were drafted into it. The circulation of the paper continued to drop and contributions fell off as many supporters rejected Day's views on the war.

Men who were drafted could file for CO status, and if their arguments were accepted by the draft board, such men would be assigned to unpaid civil public service as an alternative to military service. Men whose arguments were not accepted but who still refused to serve were sent to prison. During World War II, approximately 12,000 men were granted CO status by the U.S. selective service, but only 135 of these were Catholic. This was in part because the Church's just war theory seemed to many to be at odds with a pacifist position. It was much easier for men who belonged to the traditional "peace churches" (e.g., the Quakers and the Mennonites) to qualify for CO status for religious reasons. Some of the men associated with the Catholic Worker did receive CO status, usually forming their arguments in terms of the counsels of perfection. Alternative service was usually completed in camps around the United States, and since these men were not paid for their service, the camps were funded by churches with which the COs were affiliated. The Catholic Church, however, did not fund a camp, and Catholic COs, almost all of whom were assigned to a camp in New Hampshire, were sponsored by the meager funds of the Association of Catholic Conscientious Objectors. The ACCO was a creation of the Catholic Worker, and the camp relied on donations made to the Catholic Worker. Day visited the camp and encouraged the men in holding to their commitment. Finally, in March 1943, the Catholic Worker could not sustain this support, and these Catholic COs were sent to other camps.[32]

The most distressing event of the war for Day was the dropping of atomic bombs on two Japanese cities, Hiroshima and Nagasaki, in August 1945. In September 1945 she wrote an article denouncing "the colossal slaughter of the innocents" that resulted from the bombing. Day was appalled at the joy with which people greeted the news that America had killed so many people.

> That is, we hope we have killed them, the Associated Press, on page one, column one of the Herald Tribune, says. The effect is hoped for, not known. It is to be hoped they are vaporized, our Japanese brothers—scattered, men, women and babies, to the four winds, over the seven seas. Perhaps we will breathe their dust into our nostrils, feel them in the fog of New York on our faces, feel them in the rain on the hills of Easton [farm].[33]

Day also called for people to do penance for the use of the atomic bomb.[34] The horror and the threat of nuclear war became the focus of her pacifism as the United States moved into the era of the Cold War.

[32] For a detailed discussion of Catholic COs in World War II, see Gordon Zahn, *War, Conscience and Dissent* (New York: Hawthorn Books, 1967), chaps. 9–10.

[33] Dorothy Day, "We Go on Record: The CW Response to Hiroshima", *Catholic Worker*, September 1945, Catholic Worker Movement, http://www.catholicworker.org/dorothyday/articles/554.html.

[34] Dorothy Day, "Notes by the Way—September 1945", *Catholic Worker*, September 1945, Catholic Worker Movement website, http://www.catholicworker.org/dorothyday/articles/414.html.

The Cold War

After the Second World War, the United States and its allies entered into a state of tension, punctuated by times of open conflict, with the Soviet Union and its allies. This era, which stretched from 1945 through the breakup of the Soviet Union in the late 1980s, is known as the Cold War. One of the issues that dominated this period was the expansion of the world's nuclear arsenal and the heightened threat of nuclear war. Fear of communism gripped the United States: the Communist Party was outlawed, and communists or suspected communists were the targets of investigations and public backlash. The Catholic Church was outspoken in its criticism of communism. But Day had many friends who were communists, and she recognized that although she disagreed with much of their philosophy, they had many shared ideals in terms of social justice. In 1949, when many of the friends of her youth were being attacked as communists, Day wrote:

> I can say with warmth that I loved the people I worked with and learned much from them. They helped me to find God in His poor, in His abandoned ones, as I had not found Him in Christian churches.... I must speak from my own experience. My radical associates were the ones who were in the forefront of the struggle for a better social order where there would not be so many poor.[35]

Day herself was often accused of being a communist, and her stand caused the Catholic Worker to lose support among some people. But in her stand against nuclear war,

[35] Dorothy Day, "Beyond Politics", *Catholic Worker*, November 1949, Catholic Worker Movement website, http://www.catholicworker.org/dorothyday /articles/166.html.

she found herself confronting not only public opinion but the law.

In June 1955 the state of New York announced that there would be a statewide civil defense drill on June 15 in order to prepare for nuclear attack. During the drill, every citizen was required to take appropriate shelter in basements, fallout shelters, subway stations, and so forth, and failure to comply could result in up to a year in prison and a $500 fine.[36] Day and other pacifists decided to protest the drill because it created the illusion that nuclear war was survivable and thus thinkable. Later Day wrote: "It is not because we can say with St. Peter that we are obeying God rather than man, that we do this. There is nothing in this command of the civil defense authorities in itself against the law of God. But it is generally acknowledged that **there is no defense**. So it is a farce to pretend there is."[37] When the drill sirens went off, Day and nine others sat in a park across from city hall and refused to take shelter. They were arrested and kept in jail for twenty-four hours. The next year they did the same thing and spent five days in jail. The next year, in 1957, they protested again, and Day was sentenced to thirty days in prison. She was deeply saddened by the despair and hopelessness she encountered in so many of the women she met in prison.[38] The protests continued each year, and Day was arrested again in 1958 and 1959 but given a shorter sentence. Each year the number of protesters grew. By 1961 two thousand protesters refused

[36] Forest, *Love Is the Measure*, 97.

[37] Dorothy Day, "On Pilgrimage—July/August 1957", *Catholic Worker*, July–August 1957, Catholic Worker Movement website, http://www.catholic worker.org/dorothyday/articles/724.html. Emphasis in original.

[38] See Dorothy Day, *Loaves and Fishes* (Maryknoll, N.Y.: Orbis Books, 1997), chap. 16.

to take shelter, and the state of New York canceled any further civil defense drills.

In these acts of civil disobedience Day was still operating within the teachings of the Church. It is true that the Church stresses the importance of citizens respecting the law in order to promote the common good. But in the *Catechism* the Church also teaches:

> The citizen is obliged in conscience not to follow the directives of civil authorities when they are contrary to the demands of the moral order, to the fundamental rights of persons or the teachings of the Gospel. *Refusing obedience* to civil authorities, when their demands are contrary to those of an upright conscience, finds its justification in the distinction between serving God and serving the political community.[39]

While Day did not think that the air-raid drills themselves were morally evil, she did feel obliged to oppose preparation for nuclear war, calculated to promote the belief that such wars are winnable, because the destruction resulting from nuclear war would clearly violate the demands for moral order and the teachings of the Gospel. She endorsed acts of civil disobedience as long as those acts did not entail violence.

Though the civil defense drills ended, Day continued her writing and protests against the arms race. In September 1965, at the age of sixty-eight, she traveled to Rome just as the third and final session of the Second Vatican Council was set to open. The Council was to

---

[39] *CCC* 2242. Emphasis in original. See also "Civil Disobedience", in *Encyclopedia of Catholic Social Thought, Social Science and Social Policy*, ed. Michael Coulter, Stephen Krason, Richard Myers, and Joseph Varacalli (Lanham, Md.: Scarecrow, 2007), 194.

finalize the document *Gaudium et Spes* (Pastoral Constitution on the Church in the Modern World). Day was
part of a group of twenty Catholic women who fasted
and prayed for ten days in hopes that the Council would
issue a clear statement supporting peace and condemning
nuclear war. When the final document was released in
December, she felt her prayers had been answered, for
the document states:

> The horror and perversity of war is immensely magni-
> fied by the addition of scientific weapons. For acts of war
> involving these weapons can inflict massive and indis-
> criminate destruction, thus going far beyond the bounds
> of legitimate defense. Indeed, if the kind of instruments
> which can now be found in the armories of the great
> nations were to be employed to their fullest, an almost
> total and altogether reciprocal slaughter of each side by
> the other would follow, not to mention the widespread
> devastation that would take place in the world and the
> deadly after effects that would be spawned by the use of
> weapons of this kind....
>
> With these truths in mind, this most holy synod makes its
> own the condemnations of total war already pronounced
> by recent popes, and issues the following declaration.
>
> Any act of war aimed indiscriminately at the destruction
> of entire cities of extensive areas along with their popu-
> lation is a crime against God and man himself. It merits
> unequivocal and unhesitating condemnation.[40]

Gaudium et Spes is also the first document in which the
Church formally recognizes the legitimacy of Catholics
declaring themselves COs.[41] Day was very pleased with

[40] *Gaudium et Spes*, no. 80.
[41] Ibid., no. 79.

the document and was convinced that it would have "influence on the course of history".[42]

The Vietnam War

Day was an outspoken critic of the war in Vietnam and contrasted the U.S. involvement in the war with the works of mercy. She wrote: "The works of mercy are the opposite of the works of war, feeding the hungry, sheltering the homeless, nursing the sick, visiting the prisoner. But we are destroying crops, setting fire to entire villages and to the people in them. We are not performing the works of mercy but the works of war."[43] Day was openly critical of those Church leaders who were in favor of the war. She supported members of the Catholic Worker movement who protested and the men who burned their draft cards in protest. She was greatly distressed when one of these men, Roger LaPorte, in November 1965 poured gasoline on himself and set himself on fire at the United Nations building in protest against the war. Many people, including Thomas Merton, blamed Day and her outspoken pacifism for encouraging his death. Day refused to see his death as a suicide but rather took this "sad and terrible act" as the young man's misguided attempt to be united with and draw attention to the suffering of those in Vietnam.[44] She was also sympathetic to those whose protests against the

[42] Dorothy Day, "On Pilgrimage—December 1965", *Catholic Worker*, December 1965, Catholic Worker Movement website, http://www.catholic worker.org/dorothyday/articles/248.html.

[43] Dorothy Day, "In Peace Is My Bitterness Most Bitter", *Catholic Worker*, January 1967, Catholic Worker Movement website, http://www.catholic worker.org/dorothyday/articles/250.html.

[44] See Forest, *Love Is the Measure*, 114–16.

war took the form of destroying draft files in government offices, but she refused to support their actions because they entailed violence against another's property.

Day also had a personal stake in the war in Vietnam. Her grandson, Eric Hennessy, was drafted in 1967 and became a staff sergeant in the United States Army Rangers serving a combat tour from February to December 1969. Her prayers were always with him, and she was very grateful for his safe return from the war. But even prior to his being drafted, she had an interesting answer to those who asked whether she thought a man was in a state of mortal sin for going to war.

> I have been asked this question so often by students that I feel we must keep on trying to answer, faulty and obscure as the answer ... may seem to be. To my mind the answer lies in the realm of the motive, the intention. If a man truly thinks he is combating evil and striving for the good, if he truly thinks he is striving for the common good, he must follow his conscience regardless of others. But he always has the duty of forming his conscience by studying, listening, and being ready to hear his opponents' point of view.... The intention, they feel, is to bring about peace and initiate rational discussion around the conference table, and from there on try to establish relationships of love by building hospitals, repairing the damage done by war, restoring prosperity to a country exhausted and ravaged by war.[45]

In other words, Day recognized that it was possible for an individual to found his actions on just war principles. But she herself was never able to accept that the methods of war, and particularly those of modern war, could ever be justified.

[45] Day, "On Pilgrimage—December 1965".

Chapter Eight

DAY'S FINAL YEARS AND THE CAUSE FOR HER CANONIZATION

The final decade of Day's life saw her travel the world and gain much recognition for her life's work in the Catholic Worker. It also saw her slow down as her health declined. In a diary entry from 1972 Day reflected on her physical health and the joy she still gained from reading and study.

> No matter how old I get (and I am 75 in Nov. 1972, this year), no matter how feeble, short of breath, incapable of walking more than a few blocks, what with heart murmurs, heart failures, emphysema perhaps, arthritis in feet and knees, with all these symptoms of old age and decrepitude, my heart can still leap for joy as I read and assent to some great truth enunciated by some great mind and heart.[1]

In the early 1970s Day's health remained strong enough for her to travel a great deal. In August 1970 two priests paid for Day and another woman from the Catholic Worker to travel around the world, visiting Australia, Hong Kong, India, Tanzania, Rome, and England. While in Calcutta she

---

[1] Dorothy Day, diary entry, July 21, 1972, in *The Duty of Delight: The Diaries of Dorothy Day*, ed. Robert Ellsberg (Milwaukee, Wis.: Marquette University Press, 2008), 509.

visited for several days with Mother Teresa, who presented Day with the cross worn by her order, the Missionaries of Charity. No other layperson had ever been honored by Mother Teresa in this way.[2] Day was very moved by the witness of Mother Teresa. Day had seen poverty, sickness, and death in her years in New York but never on the scale she witnessed in Calcutta. (After this initial meeting in Calcutta, Mother Teresa visited with Day several times when she came to New York.) In 1971 Day traveled to Eastern Europe and Russia, and in 1973 she traveled to England, Northern Ireland, and the republic of Ireland.

In the summer of 1973 the singer Joan Baez invited Day to come to California to spend a week with the Institute for the Study of Nonviolence. Day accepted the invitation and arrived in California at the end of July. While she was there she accompanied Cesar Chavez and the United Farm Workers as they picketed the fruit orchards to protest the treatment of migrant workers. During one of these protests, on August 2, Day was arrested for the final time in her life, along with 140 other protesters, including thirty nuns and two priests. Day and the others spent nearly two weeks in what was basically a prison farm for the detainees, until the charges were dropped.

In the spring of 1975, at the age of seventy-seven, Day announced that she was stepping down from running the day-to-day activities of the *Catholic Worker*, though she continued to write for the paper. She wrote that in her retirement she wanted to develop her prayer life and "grow in the life of the spirit".[3] In August 1976 Day made

[2] Jim Forest, *Love Is the Measure: A Biography of Dorothy Day* (Maryknoll, N.Y.: Orbis Books, 1986), 125.

[3] Dorothy Day, "On Pilgrimage—March/April 1975", *Catholic Worker*, Catholic Worker Movement website, http://www.catholicworker.org/dorothyday /articles/548.html.

her last speaking trip to the Eucharistic congress in Philadelphia. The date for her talk was August 6, the Feast of the Transfiguration and the anniversary of the bombing of Hiroshima. In her talk she emphasized the importance of penance as preparation for the reception of the Eucharist. She said: "It is a fearful thought that unless we do penance we will perish. Our creator gave us life, and the Eucharist to sustain our life. But we have given the world instruments of death of inconceivable magnitude."[4] After the congress, Day traveled to Pittsburgh for a weeklong retreat with Father John Hugo (see pp. 98–100). Soon after returning to New York, Day suffered a heart attack, from which she never fully recovered, and this greatly reduced her activity in her final years.

Day spent her last years mostly confined to Maryhouse, the Catholic Worker house in New York City, with occasional trips to Staten Island and the Catholic Worker farm in Tivoli, New York, when her health permitted. In June 1977 she wrote:

When I was praying the Our Father and the Hail Mary this morning, it suddenly occurred to me how good it was to end our prayer to Mary with "now and at the hour of our death." I don't think I had realized how often we pray for the hour of our death, that it would be a good one. It is good, certainly, to have a long period of "ill health" ... nothing specific, mild but frightening pains in the heart, and sickness, ebb-tide, ebbing of life, and then some days of strength and creativity.[5]

<hr />

[4] Quoted in Forest, *Love Is the Measure*, 135.

[5] Dorothy Day, "On Pilgrimage—June 1977", *Catholic Worker*, June 1977, Catholic Worker Movement website, http://www.catholicworker.org/dorothy day/articles/578.html.

Because her health made writing difficult, she was less involved with the newspaper and spent more of her time reading and rereading some of her favorite novels. She still loved the Russian authors Tolstoy and Dostoyevsky, whom she discovered as a girl. She enjoyed visits from her friends; her daughter, Tamar; her nine grandchildren; and her thirteen great-grandchildren. Forster Batterham and Day kept in regular touch with each other as they both neared the end of their lives. They spoke on the phone almost daily. On some evenings Tamar and Forster would visit Day in her room at the Catholic Worker house, the three of them chatting and watching TV together.[6] Though she usually could not get to Mass, a volunteer brought her Holy Communion every day.

In the fall of 1980, after a brief stay in the hospital, Day returned to Maryhouse for the last time. On Saturday, November 29, 1980, on the eve of the First Sunday of Advent, Dorothy Day quietly and peacefully died with Tamar by her side. She was eighty-three years old. Michael Harank, a friend who was at the house, remembered this about the day she died: "She had spoken to me about how grateful she was to be able to be with her own mother when she had died, and I think her only wish, really, was that her daughter could be with her when she herself died. And Tamar was there. That prayer was answered."[7] Day was laid out in Maryhouse in a simple pine coffin. On the day of the funeral, grandchildren served as her pallbearers and carried the coffin to a crowded Nativity Church around the corner. Tamar, Forster Batterham, and Day's brother John walked behind the coffin, followed by a procession

---

[6] Rosalie Riegle, *Dorothy Day: Portraits by Those Who Knew Her* (Maryknoll, N.Y.: Orbis Books, 2003), 160. Batterham passed away in 1985.

[7] Quoted ibid., 181.

of friends. Harank, who carried the Paschal candle in the procession, remembered a telling moment from that walk:

> Just as we were turning the corner, this man came running up. He was quite disheveled, and clearly, not in his right mind in some ways, and he just dashed up to the casket. Ordinarily, one would think that when something like this would happen, there would be chaos and panic. But I think the grandchildren who were carrying the casket knew that this man was in many ways symbolic of the friends of Dorothy throughout the years. He was poor and homeless and suffering from mental illness. The grandchildren stopped, which was a very moving thing, and I remember he went right up to the casket and simply touched it. It was over very quickly, but you could see people were nervous about what was happening. But all he did was go up, touch it, and then he left. One of the "ambassadors of Christ," as Peter [Maurin] used to call them.[8]

Day was buried in a donated grave in Resurrection Cemetery on Staten Island, within walking distance of the beach house where her conversion had occurred.[9] As her body was lowered into the ground, Forster Batterham took a rose from one of the floral arrangements and tossed it into the grave.[10] The Dominican priest who gave the homily at her funeral described the scene at the graveside this way:

> As we were placing the coffin into the ground, three greyhound dogs suddenly appeared, frolicking and dancing around, an almost playful relief to the solemn moment, the final moment. With a trowel I put dirt onto the coffin and turned to a Dominican colleague, Fr. Regis Ryan.

[8] Quoted ibid., 185.
[9] Forest, *Love Is the Measure*, 146.
[10] Riegle, *Dorothy Day*, 187.

"The greyhounds!" I knew he caught the uncanny sym-
bolism. A greyhound with a torch is a symbol of the
Dominican Order, "the dogs of the Lord." It's a play on
the Latin words *Domini canes*. Three stands for the Trinity, of course. And Dorothy often recounted how Eugene
O'Neill in a drunken stupor could recite to her Francis
Thompson's "The Hound of Heaven." In *The Long Loneliness* she wrote that all of her life she had been haunted,
hounded by God. At the grave site I thought, she's no
longer "hounded." Instead, the hounds were dancing,
rejoicing in celebration. Dorothy was home.[11]

Day's gravestone bears this simple inscription:

Dorothy Day
November 8, 1897—November 29, 1980
Deo Gratias.

The Cause for Her Canonization

There was much speculation after Day's death about
whether she would be recognized as a saint by the Church.
In an oft-quoted line, in response to a reporter's reference
to her as a saint, Day said: "Don't call me a saint; I don't
want to be dismissed that easily."[12] But this statement
should not be misunderstood as a rejection of the canonization process. What she meant by this is that too often,
when we identify someone as a saint, we think that they
are so different from us that we do not recognize that
we are all called to be saints. When Day rejected being
called a saint, she was rejecting the notion that a few saints
bear all the responsibility of living the message of the

[11] Geffrey Gneuhs, quoted ibid., 188.
[12] Ibid., 193.

Gospels in the world while the rest of us do not need to worry about it. Many of her friends and admirers were very supportive of the movement for her canonization. Others of her friends were opposed to beginning the canonization process because they feared that her radical message would be lost if she was "institutionalized" as a saint. Still others argued that Day herself would be opposed to canonization because of the cost involved, money that would be better spent feeding the poor.

In November 1997, on the one hundredth anniversary of her birth, John Cardinal O'Connor, then archbishop of New York, formally proposed going forward with Dorothy Day's cause for canonization. In his homily that Sunday, he emphasized Day's love of the poor and her faithfulness to the Church. He also acknowledged her willingness to be critical of the Church when it failed in its mission. The cardinal emphasized Day's life as holding a special meaning for women who have suffered an abortion.

> I wish every woman who has ever suffered an abortion (including perhaps someone or several in this church) would come to know Dorothy Day. Her story was so typical. Made pregnant by a man who insisted she have an abortion, who then abandoned her anyway, she suffered terribly from what she had done, and later pleaded with others not to do the same. But later, too, after becoming a Catholic, she learned the love and mercy of the Lord, and she knew she never had to worry about His forgiveness. (This is why I have never condemned a woman who has had an abortion; I weep with her and ask her to remember Dorothy Day's sorrow but to know always God's loving mercy and forgiveness.)[13]

[13] John O'Connor, "On the Idea of Sainthood and Dorothy Day", homily, St. Patrick's Cathedral, New York City, November 9, 1997; *Catholic New York*, November 13, 1997, 13–14; Catholic Worker Movement website, http://www.catholicworker.org/pages/o'connor-sainthood-homily.html.

Cardinal O'Connor rejected the idea that Day should not be put forward for canonization because some of her views were un-American. He also rejected the views of those who claimed that canonization would be an attempt to sanitize some of her more radical views. The cardinal thought that both sides failed to understand why the Church canonizes a saint. He asked:

> But why does the Church canonize saints? In part that their person, their works, their lives will become that much better known and that they will encourage others to follow in their footsteps. And, of course, that the Church may say formally and officially—"This is sanctity, this is the road to eternal life, to feed the hungry, to clothe the naked, to house the homeless, to love every human person made in the image and likeness of God."[14]

In the March 2000 issue, Cardinal O'Connor was happy to announce that the Vatican had approved the opening of Day's cause: "It is with great joy that I announce the approval of the Holy See for the Archdiocese of New York to open the Cause for the Beatification and Canonization of Dorothy Day. With this approval comes the title Servant of God. What a gift to the Church in New York and the Church Universal this is."[15] In this same article he explained that Church dogmatists, moralists, and canonists had carefully examined all of Day's post-conversion writings and found them to be in complete fidelity to the Church.

[14] Ibid.

[15] John O'Connor, "Dorothy Day's Sainthood Cause Begins", *Catholic Worker*, March 2000; *Catholic New York*, March 16, 2000; Catholic Worker Movement website, http://www.catholicworker.org/pages/o'connor-cause -begins.html.

Cardinal O'Connor used this occasion to speak again of Day's particular place as a model for women agonizing because of abortion.

To be sure, her life is a model for all in the third millennium, but especially for women who have had or are considering abortions. It is a well-known fact that Dorothy Day procured an abortion before her conversion to the Faith. She regretted it every day of her life. After her conversion from a life akin to that of the pre-converted Augustine of Hippo, she proved a stout defender of human life. The conversion of mind and heart that she exemplified speaks volumes to all women today on two fronts. First, it demonstrates the mercy of God, mercy in that a woman who sinned so gravely could find such unity with God upon conversion. Second, it demonstrates that one may turn from the ultimate act of violence against innocent life in the womb to a position of total holiness and pacifism. In short, I contend that her abortion should not preclude her cause, but intensifies it.[16]

Rome's approval allowed the Archdiocese of New York to continue pursuing the cause of Day's canonization, and in July 2005 O'Connor's successor, Edward Cardinal Egan, announced the establishment of the Guild for Dorothy Day, which currently pursues the cause of Day's beatification and canonization. In putting his support behind Day's cause, Cardinal Egan said:

Dorothy Day sought no accolades. She dismissed any suggestion that she was a saint, though she took extraordinary delight in studying the lives of the saints. She accepted the rejection of certain women's groups who could not

[16] Ibid.

forgive her condemnation of abortion, just as she accepted the rejection of a great number of her followers who could not understand her uncompromising commitment to peace. She told Church leaders in no uncertain terms when she thought they were mistaken in matters of social policy, but stood foursquare with them in matters of faith and morals.[17]

The Catholic Worker Movement Today

The death of Dorothy Day did not mark the end of the Catholic Worker movement. Today approximately two hundred Catholic Worker houses and farms operate around the United States and in several other countries around the world. All Catholic Worker communities continue to support the needy and to proclaim a message of peace and justice. Many of them no longer identify themselves with or support the teachings of the Catholic Church. But others follow closely the spirit and teachings of Dorothy Day and Peter Maurin and recognize the essential connection between their work and the Church.

[17] Edward Egan, " 'Saint Dorothy'?", July 7, 2007, Archdiocese of New York website, http://archny.org/news/saint-dorothy.

BIBLIOGRAPHY

Works by Dorothy Day

All the Way to Heaven: The Selected Letters of Dorothy Day. Edited by Robert Ellsberg. Milwaukee, Wis.: Marquette University Press, 2010.

"Catholic Peace Fellowship Statement on Abortion". By Dorothy Day, et al. June 28, 1974. Consistent Life Network website. http://media.wix.com/ugd/7f0bd5_814bb37aa8 ef483691670fe0a9f3fee7.pdf.

Catholic Worker. [Various articles.] 1933–1977. Catholic Worker Movement website. http://www.catholicworker.org /dorothyday/.

Dorothy Day: Selected Writings. Edited by Robert Ellsberg. Maryknoll, N.Y.: Orbis Books, 1993.

Dorothy Day: Writings from "Commonweal". Edited by Patrick Jordan. Collegeville, Minn.: Liturgical Press, 2002.

The Duty of Delight: The Diaries of Dorothy Day. Edited by Robert Ellsberg. Milwaukee, Wis.: Marquette University Press, 2008.

The Eleventh Virgin. New York: Albert and Charles Boni, 1924.

From Union Square to Rome. Maryknoll, N.Y.: Orbis Books, 2006.

House of Hospitality. New York: Sheed and Ward, 1939.

Loaves and Fishes. Maryknoll, N.Y.: Orbis Books, 2007.

The Long Loneliness. New York: Harper and Brothers, 1952.

On Pilgrimage. Grand Rapids, Mich.: Wm. B. Eerdmans, 1999.

Peter Maurin: Apostle to the World. With Francis J. Sicius. Maryknoll, N.Y.: Orbis Books, 2004.

"Reflections during Advent". Pt. 3, "Chastity". *Ave Maria*, December 10, 1966. Catholic Worker Movement website.

http://www.catholicworker.org/dorothyday/articles
/561.html.

"Reflections during Advent". Pt. 4, "Obedience". *Ave Maria*, December 17, 1966. Catholic Worker Movement website.
http://www.catholicworker.org/dorothyday/articles
/562.html.

Therese. Notre Dame, Ind.: Fides Publishers Association, 1960.

Works about Dorothy Day and the
Catholic Worker Movement

Anglada, Eric. "Taking Root: The History and New Growth
of Catholic Worker Farms". *America*, May 6, 2013, 13–15.

Catoir, John T. *Encounters with Holiness*. New York: Society of
St. Paul, 2007.

Cavanaugh, William T. "Dorothy Day and the Mystical Body of
Christ in the Second World War." In *Dorothy Day and the
Catholic Worker Movement: Centenary Essays*, edited by Wil-
liam Thorn, Phillip Runkel, and Susan Mountain, 458–64.
Milwaukee, Wis.: Marquette University Press, 2001.

Coles, Robert. *Dorothy Day: A Radical Devotion*. Boston: Da
Capo Press, 1987.

Egan, Edward. "'Saint Dorothy'?", July 7, 2007. Archdiocese of
New York website. http://archny.org/news/saint-dorothy.

Forest, Jim. *All Is Grace: A Biography of Dorothy Day*. Maryknoll,
N.Y.: Orbis Books, 2012.

———. *Love Is the Measure: A Biography of Dorothy Day*. Maryknoll, N.Y.: Orbis Books, 1986.

Lange, Alice. "Dorothy Day on Women's Right to Choose".
Houston Catholic Worker website. http://cjd.org/2008
/06/01/dorothy-day-on-womens-right-to-choose/.

LeBrun, John L. "The Way of Love: Pacifism and the Catholic Worker Movement, 1933–1939". In *Dorothy Day and
the Catholic Worker Movement: Centenary Essays*, edited
by William Thorn, Phillip Runkel, and Susan Mountin,
465–73. Milwaukee, Wis.: Marquette University Press,
2001.

Maurin, Peter. *Easy Essays*. Chicago: Franciscan Herald, 1977.

Merriman, Brigid O'Shea. *Searching for Christ: The Spirituality of Dorothy Day*. Notre Dame, Ind.: University of Notre Dame Press, 1994.

Miller, William D. *All Is Grace: The Spirituality of Dorothy Day*. Garden City, N.Y.: Doubleday, 1987.

——. *Dorothy Day: A Biography*. San Francisco: Harper and Row, 1982.

O'Connor, John. "On the Idea of Sainthood and Dorothy Day". Homily, St. Patrick's Cathedral, New York City, November 9, 1997. *Catholic New York*, November 13, 1997, 13–14. Catholic Worker Movement website. http://www.catholicworker.org/pages/o'connor-sainthood-homily.html.

Riegle, Rosalie. *Dorothy Day: Portraits by Those Who Knew Her*. Maryknoll, N.Y.: Orbis Books, 2003.

Zwick, Mark and Louise. *The Catholic Worker Movement: Intellectual and Spiritual Origins*. New York: Paulist, 2005.

Other Works

Augustine. *The City of God*. Translated by Gerald Walsh and Daniel Honan. Vol. 3. Fathers of the Church 24. New York: Fathers of the Church, 1954.

——. *The City of God*. Translated by Gerald Walsh and Grace Monahan. Vol. 2. Fathers of the Church 24. New York: Fathers of the Church, 1952.

Benedict. *The Rule of Saint Benedict in English*. Edited by Timothy Fry. New York: Vintage Books, 1998.

Benedict XVI. *Deus Caritas Est: On Christian Love*. 2005. Holy See website. http://w2.vatican.va/content/benedict-xvi/en/encyclicals/documents/hf_ben-xvi_enc_20051225_deus-caritas-est.html.

Catechism of the Catholic Church. 2nd ed. Vatican City: Libreria Editrice Vaticana; Washington, D.C.: United States Catholic Conference, 2000.

Chesterton, G. K. *Irish Impressions*. Norfolk, Va.: IHS, 2002.

————. *The Outline of Sanity*. London: Meuthen, 1928.

Coulter, Michael, Stephen Krason, Richard Myers, and Joseph Varacalli, eds. *Encyclopedia of Catholic Social Thought, Social Science and Social Policy*. Lanham, Md.: Scarecrow, 2007.

Francis. *Evangelii Gaudium*. 2013. Holy See website. http://w2 .vatican.va/content/francesco/en/apost_exhortations /documents/papa-francesco_esortazione-ap_20131124 _evangelii-gaudium.html.

John Paul II. Address to UNIV '99 Congress of University Students, March 30, 1999. Holy See website. http://w2 .vatican.va/content/john-paul-ii/en/speeches/1999 /march/documents/hf_jp-ii_spe_19990330_univ-99 .html.

————. *Centesimus Annus: On the Hundredth Anniversary of "Rerum Novarum"*. 1991. Holy See website. http://w2 .vatican.va/content/john-paul-ii/en/encyclicals/docu ments/hf_jp-ii_enc_01051991_centesimus-annus.html.

————. *Dives in Misericordia*. 1980. Holy See website. http:// w2.vatican.va/content/john-paul-ii/en/encyclicals /documents/hf_jp-ii_enc_30111980_dives-in-miseri cordia.html.

————. *Dominum et Vivificantem: On the Holy Spirit in the Life of the Church and the World*. 1986. Holy See website. http:// w2.vatican.va/content/john-paul-ii/en/encyclicals /documents/hf_jp-ii_enc_18051986_dominum-et -vivificantem.html.

————. *Fides et Ratio: On the Relationship between Faith and Reason*. 1998. Holy See website. http://w2.vatican.va /content/john-paul-ii/en/encyclicals/documents/hf _jp-ii_enc_14091998_fides-et-ratio.html.

————. *Novo Millennio Ineunte: At the Close of the Great Jubi- lee of the Year 2000*. 2001. Holy See website. http://w2 .vatican.va/content/john-paul-ii/en/apost_letters/2001 /documents/hf_jp-ii_apl_20010106_novo-millennio-in eunte.html.

————. *Sollicitudo Rei Socialis*. 1987. Holy See website. http:// w2.vatican.va/content/john-paul-ii/en/encyclicals

/documents/hf_jp-ii_enc_30121987_sollicitudo-rei
-socialis.html.

————. *Veritatis Splendor.* 1993. Holy See website. http://
w2.vatican.va/content/john-paul-ii/en/encyclicals
/documents/hf_jp-ii_enc_06081993_veritatis-splendor
.html.

Leo XIII. *Rerum Novarum.* 1891. Holy See website. http://w2
.vatican.va/content/leo-xiii/en/encyclicals/documents
/hf_l-xiii_enc_15051891_rerum-novarum.html.

Maritain, Jacques. *The Person and the Common Good.* Translated by John Fitzgerald. Notre Dame, Ind.: University of
Notre Dame Press, 2002.

Marx, Karl, and Friedrich Engels. *Manifesto of the Communist Party.* In *The Marx-Engels Reader,* 2nd ed., edited by
Robert Tucker, 469–500. New York: W.W. Norton,
1978.

Michel, Virgil. *Christian Social Construction.* Milwaukee, Wis.:
Bruce, 1937.

Mounier, Emmanuel. *Personalism.* Translated by Philip Mairet.
Notre Dame, Ind.: University of Notre Dame Press, 1970.

————. *Révolution personaliste et communautaire.* In *Œuvres,* vol. 1,
1931–1939. Paris: Éditions du Seuil, 1961.

Pius XI. *Quadragesimo Anno.* 1931. Holy See website. http://w2
.vatican.va/content/pius-xi/en/encyclicals/documents
/hf_p-xi_enc_19310515_quadragesimo-anno.html.

————. *Rite Expiatis.* 1926. Holy See website. http://w2.vatican
.va/content/pius-xi/en/encyclicals/documents/hf_p-xi
_enc_30041926_rite-expiatis.html.

Pontifical Council for Justice and Peace. *Compendium of the
Social Doctrine of the Church.* Washington, D.C.: United
States Conference of Catholic Bishops, 2005.

Thomas Aquinas. *Summa Theologiae.* Translated by the English
Dominican Fathers. New York: Benziger Brothers, 1948.

United States Conference of Catholic Bishops. *A Century of
Social Teaching: A Common Heritage, a Continuing Challenge.*
Washington, D.C.: United States Catholic Conference,
1990.

————. "In All Things Charity: A Pastoral Challenge for the New Millennium". November 18, 1999. United States Conference of Catholic Bishops website. http://www.usccb.org/about/catholic-campaign-for-human-development/in-all III:16 (November 18, 1999)

Vatican II. *Dignitatis Humanae: Declaration on Religious Liberty.* December 7, 1965. Holy See website. http://www.vatican.va/archive/hist_councils/ii_vatican_council/documents/vat-ii_decl_19651207_dignitatis-humanae_en.html.

————. *Gaudium et Spes: Pastoral Constitution on the Church in the Modern World.* December 7, 1965. Holy See website. http://www.vatican.va/archive/hist_councils/ii_vatican_council/documents/vat-ii_cons_19651207_gaudium-et-spes_en.html

Zahn, Gordon. *War, Conscience and Dissent.* New York: Hawthorn Books, 1967.

INDEX